Praise for
In Growth We Trust

"... written with clarity, compassion, and concern for our future. It deserves to be carefully read by every conscientious city, county, state, and national planner."

H.E. Scheiblich,
Elgin, South Carolina

"... an extremely well reasoned and data-based argument for population stabilization."

Harry Levins,
Advocates for a Sustainable Albemarle Population,
Charlottesville, Virginia

"... extremely professional ... thoughtful, careful ..."

Nick Carter, Ecologist
Greensboro, Maryland

"... a well written document that has a wealth of good information in it."

Bob DeGroot, President,
Maryland Alliance for Greenway Improvements and Conservation,
Rockville, Maryland

"It ought to be in the hands of every local environmentalist."

Armin Behr,
Bethesda, Maryland

Abbreviations

APF	Adequate Public Facilities
COG	Metropolitan Washington Council of Governments
EF	Ecological Footprint
EWTP	Potomac Estuary Experimental Wastewater Treatment Plant
IAW	In accordance with
NRT	Nitrogen Reduction Technology
PAS	Principal Arterial Street
TFR	Total Fertility Rate: Average number of children born during a woman's lifetime, based on current birth statistics.
TTI	Texas Transportation Institute
UOSA	Upper Occoquan Sewage Authority
VMT	Vehicle Miles Traveled
WMA	Washington Metropolitan Area
WMATA	Washington Metropolitan Area Transit Authority

Front cover geographic depictions from USGS,
(http://edcwww2.cr.usgs.gov/umap/htmls/ftp.html)

In Growth We Trust

Sprawl, Smart Growth, and Rapid Population Growth

Edwin Stennett

GEM Report No. 1
July 2002

Growth Education Movement, Inc.
Gaithersburg, Maryland

Thanks: The author wishes to thank all those who provided encouragement, support, and feedback during preparation of this publication. Special thanks are extended to: Anne Ambler, Armin Behr, Nick Carter, Bob DeGroot, Jim Fary, John Fay, Crystal Heshmat, Tom Horton, Betsy Johnson, Ron LaCoss, Dan Lynch, Norm Meadows, Ed Merrifield, Mason Olcott, Jon Robinson, Cliff Terry, Wolfger Schneider, and Joan Willey. Very special thanks to my wife, Beverly, who so often provided vital feedback in her role as a "focus group of one."

Published by: Growth Education Movement, Inc. The Growth Education Movement is an independent 501(c)(3) tax-exempt corporation. Its mission is to make people aware that:
- failing to address U.S. population growth will increasingly diminish the quality of life of our children and grandchildren,
- our mushrooming population is neither inevitable nor economically necessary, and
- U.S. population stabilization can be achieved by voluntary means supported by the vast majority of Americans.

To learn more or order a copy of this book, please visit:
www.growtheducation.org.

Requests to reprint all or part of *In Growth We Trust* should be addressed to:

Growth Education Movement, Inc.
P.O. Box 2876
Gaithersburg, Maryland 20886-2876

This book was printed in Gaithersburg, Maryland using recycled paper.

2nd printing, 2004

Copyright © 2002 by Growth Education Movement, Inc.
ISBN 0-9723615-0-2

Table of Contents

A Vital and Attainable Change 1

Growth Pains 8

    Sprawl and Vanishing Open Space 8
    Road Congestion 16
    Water Worries 29
    Treasure the Chesapeake 38

Growth Pressures 47

    Washington Area Population Growth 47
    National Population Growth 50
    Choices 54

Growth and Economic Wellbeing 56

    Local Job Growth and Local Unemployment 56
    Population Growth and Economic Growth 59
    An Ethical Threshold 64

Growth Politics 68

Toward a Better Future 76

    Restraining the Growth Machine 76
    Confronting Our National Population Growth 86

A Life-Changing Event 100

Appendices 106

    Appendix A – Growth Machine Organizations 106

Appendix B – Population Projection Information *110*
Appendix C – Dependency Ratios *115*
Appendix D – Declining Per Capita VMT Growth *120*

Endnotes **124**

1
A Vital and Attainable Change

Urban sprawl is a significant and growing concern for Americans. Articles about sprawl and measures to combat it appear almost daily in both major and local newspapers. More than two dozen books have been written about it within the last ten years, and several hundred anti-sprawl proposals have been decided at state and local ballot boxes in recent elections.

From Maryland's Smart Growth policies to Oregon's famed Urban Growth Boundaries, people all across America are watching the efforts to rein in the urban sprawl that is altering landscapes and quality of life all across our nation. While the emphasis may vary from state to state, all of the efforts are similar. Key strategies include:

- encouraging redevelopment of inner cities, and promoting in-fill of suburban properties skipped over by previous sprawl;
- building increased public transit capacity, and encouraging high-density development around public transit facilities;
- encouraging mixed use developments so as to reduce vehicular dependence, and
- preserving vanishing green-space through zoning, purchase of development rights, or outright purchase of property.

In general these efforts enjoy popular support, but they also meet intense opposition from developers, real estate brokers, land speculators, and ordinary citizens concerned about the impact on their property. Such opposition has always been part of the Smart Growth movement, and much effort has been devoted to overcoming it – including efforts to harmonize the interests of the larger community with the special interests.

2 In Growth We Trust

Recently some Smart Growth proponents have begun to recognize that special interest opposition is not the only threat to the success of Smart Growth. With the benefit of almost thirty years of hindsight it is becoming clear that the usual Smart Growth tools are not sufficient in regions experiencing rapid population growth. For example, Oregon has had its growth boundaries since 1973, but sprawl still eats up the land in the Willamette Valley. The reason is that the boundaries are not fixed but expand with the population – and the population of the Willamette Valley is exploding.[1] In April of 2001 the Willamette Valley Livability Forum noted that "by 2050, urban growth boundaries in the Willamette Valley will grow by 106,000 acres – an area equivalent to about 160 downtown Portlands."[2]

Public acknowledgement of the linkage between rapid population growth and sprawl is not yet widespread. For example, the July 2001 issue of *National Geographic Magazine* contains a 26-page feature article on urban sprawl. With flowing text and its hallmark photographs, the magazine depicts urban sprawl across the land. The article has one salient characteristic that echoes nearly all of the anti-sprawl efforts across the country – *the option of addressing the population growth that drives much of the sprawl is not mentioned.*

It is unlikely that the author of the *National Geographic* piece is unaware of the link between population growth and sprawl. The everyday experience of anyone who has lived a decade or more in a rapidly growing metropolitan area abounds with evidence that swelling numbers of people contribute substantially to both our sprawl and our traffic congestion.

We will not second guess the author's silence here, but observe that he may have given us a glimpse of his true feeling in the way that he chose to end the article. His closing paragraph is as follows:

A Vital and Attainable Change

> *"Then I heard another voice. It was Tracy Molitors', speaking to my memory of our meeting in a kitchen in Mason, Ohio. I had asked her where this national experience called sprawl was going to end. And she said, 'End? Why there's no end in sight, the way it's going. We just keep moving farther and farther out until one of these days we'll all be rubbing elbows. All the way across America.'"*[3]

While almost no anti-sprawl organizations advocate confronting the population growth that drives much of the sprawl, a change may be "in the wind." Last year a leading anti-sprawl voice, the Sierra Club, acknowledged that "no matter how smart the growth or how good the planning, a rapid increase in population can overwhelm a community's best efforts."[4]

Re-conceptualizing the sprawl issue, recognizing that Smart Growth efforts must be augmented with efforts to address our mushrooming population, are changes that this report seeks to encourage. We begin by illustrating that rapid population growth in the Washington region is a major cause of sprawl and traffic congestion in the area, and that our best Smart Growth efforts will be overwhelmed if we do not stabilize our regional population.

The information illustrating that Washington area Smart Growth efforts are unlikely to produce the desired results (if we do not slow our population growth) is included only to illustrate the necessity of broadening our attack on sprawl. No criticism of Smart Growth per se is implied. Indeed, this report was written with a little "home-state pride" in the fact that Maryland leads the nation in land preservation by means of purchase of development rights, and that Montgomery County, Maryland is nationally renowned for its transfer of development rights program.[5]

While the focus of this report is the Washington area, the message applies to all metropolitan areas experiencing similar population growth. If you live in any of the many high population growth areas in the U.S., this report will help you see the consequences of failing to address the population issue, and it will help you understand the various steps that will lead to a better future.

As we shall see subsequently, metropolitan area population growth can be slowed by ending subsidies that promote local population growth. This will not be an easy task because there are wealthy and well organized special interests who profit from local growth: land speculators, developers, real estate brokers, newspapers, etc. Neither should it be an impossible task, if enough of the general citizenry demand what is best for the community as a whole.

Of course, if our national population continues to grow rapidly, success in curbing sprawl in one region simply portends more sprawl in other regions. Thus, conquering sprawl over the entire country requires that we work toward national population stabilization.

Though special interests are involved, ending our national population growth is not just a case of the general citizenry against the special interests. It is a more complex matter involving all of us with our many different perspectives on the subjects of procreation and immigration. It is also a matter of education and awareness. For example, many Americans are unaware that both our population growth rate and our fertility rate (average number of children born per woman) are much higher than those in virtually all other developed nations.

Among Americans who are aware of our rapid population growth and its consequences, some believe that stabilizing the U.S. population is not possible if net immigration continues at current levels (somewhat less than 1 million per year[6]). But as we shall see in Chapter 6 of this report, a stable U.S. population

A Vital and Attainable Change

can be achieved through a modest reduction in U.S. fertility, *even with an annual net immigration of 1 million people.*

Achieving a modest reduction in fertility in no way means use of coercive tactics – or criticizing people who choose to have three or more children. It means educating all Americans about the benefits of lower fertility. It means recognizing the role that poverty plays and aiding those in need. This report advocates a variety of fertility reduction approaches that benefit affected individuals as well as our society. One obvious approach is increased reproductive health care for low-income people. Increased access to this needed service means fewer unintended pregnancies, fewer abortions, and healthier babies.

In our modern high-tech society, most people naturally opt for small families when they feel that they and their children can fully participate in the economic fruits of the society. In much of the industrialized world outside the U.S., this tendency has resulted in astonishingly low fertility rates. Among fourteen industrialized nations the total fertility rate ranges from a high of 1.85 (Norway) to a low of 1.15 (Spain).[7] All but Norway already have a fertility rate below the value that we need in order to stabilize the population of the U.S.

Preventing population growth from overwhelming our Smart Growth efforts is a less formidable task than most people suppose. On the other hand, there is one obstacle that stands out from all others: our profound reticence to discussing the population component of the sprawl problem. This reticence exists even though, when asked directly, a large majority of Americans (77%) respond that overpopulation of the United States is either a major problem now or likely to be a problem in the future.[8] Reluctance to consider the population issue is a serious obstacle to curbing sprawl, and it must be overcome. It is imperative that Americans end their avoidance of the issue, and move it onto the national "radar screen."

The key to this transition already exists. Population growth is often seen as a problem for the future, and it is human nature to pay more attention to an immediate problem than to a distant one. But it is also human nature to care about those who follow us. We all want our children and their descendents to enjoy a healthy environment, clean air and water, uncluttered land, ample open space, natural beauty, wilderness, and abundant wildlife. It is this caring about our children's lives that is the key to getting people to confront the population problem.

While this caring provides the opportunity for change, the instrument of change is education. We need to make people aware that population growth is neither inevitable nor economically necessary. We need to make people aware that U.S. population stabilization can be achieved by voluntary means supported by the vast majority of Americans; and we need to make people aware that advocacy for U.S. population stabilization is clearly in the interests of our future and our children.

Increasing public awareness is *the* goal of this report. The report focuses on five areas:

- *growth pains* – examples of Washington area quality of life and environmental costs that result from excessive population growth;
- *growth pressures* – the demographic projections that inform us about the magnitude of growth problems we face;
- *growth and economic wellbeing* – some misconceptions about the importance of population growth to our individual economic wellbeing;
- *growth politics* – the forces, known collectively as the **Growth Machine**, that promote population growth in every locality across the country; and

A Vital and Attainable Change

- *a better future* – some practical steps that we can take to arrest the quality of life declines caused by continued population growth.

In general, public demand necessarily precedes governmental action. While this report advocates measures to facilitate a modest, voluntary fertility reduction, this advocacy cannot take root in state and Federal policies until mainstream America is educated and ready to demand a change. Therefore, first and foremost, the goal of this report is to inform in order to help create a public demand for change. Several years may be required, but with a growing number of informed people, the problem of population growth will ultimately make its appearance on the national "radar screen." Only then will Congress or state legislatures consider expenditures for facilitating population stabilization. Only then will Smart Growth efforts be able to provide a full and lasting benefit for our children and grandchildren.

2

Growth Pains

Sprawl and Vanishing Open Space

"We used to go out Route 50 for a drive in the country. Now, it's strip mall, town houses and apartments, one after the other. Pretty soon there won't be any open space between here and Winchester." (Madelon Vorbau, Annandale, Virginia)[9]

What Ms. Vorbau is reacting to, what many of us in the Washington area are reacting to, is graphically portrayed in the illustration on the cover of this report. We are losing vast amounts of open space and forests. We are losing an important connection with the natural world. And with the destruction of open space and forests we are polluting our air and streams, and jeopardizing the Chesapeake Bay. According to the Chesapeake Bay Foundation, continuation of our sprawl patterns "will overwhelm progress made to date to improve the health of the Chesapeake and the quality of life throughout the watershed."[10]

The fact that we are degrading our quality of life and our environment has not gone unnoticed. In November 2000 a survey of residents in the Potomac watershed indicated that more than half of the respondents felt that development has caused the quality of life to decline in the region.[11] In late December of 2000 and early January of 2001, a *Baltimore Sun* poll indicated that there is so much concern about our local environment that 68% of Maryland voters felt that the state should work hard to protect the environment, *even if it might cost some jobs.*[12]

Growth Pains

As sprawl is a major concern for the Washington area, so it is for much of the nation. A few decades ago the noun "sprawl" didn't exist in our national lexicon. Today, the term is so commonplace that it is virtually on the tip of our national tongue. In 1998, Colorado residents rated growth [sprawl] their number one problem.[13] Nationally, some 240 anti-sprawl ballot initiatives were voted on in November 1998.[14] In November 2000, there were 553 state and local growth related ballot measures.[15] And between January 1, 1996 and January 1, 2001, the term sprawl was mentioned in 1,565 *Washington Post* articles.[16] On average this is six articles per week!

Symptoms of Sprawl

Sprawl is a malady that presents multiple symptoms; for example:

- decay of central city and inner suburban areas coincident with flight to the outer suburbs and beyond,
- single use suburban development patterns that force reliance on automobiles for access to every essential place: work, shopping, schools, recreation, medical services, etc.,
- a landscape with a measles like appearance and high per capita infrastructure costs due to development occurring "willy-nilly" in disconnected pockets,
- vanishing open space.

The first three symptoms are outside the scope of this report. They are little related to population growth, and are being effectively targeted by Smart Growth efforts. Our focus will be on the fourth symptom.

Smart Growth measures target vanishing open space by encouraging compact development and discouraging subsidies for profligate land use. In areas of the country experiencing little or no population growth, measures such as these may be the only ones required to keep open space from vanishing. But in the Washington area and other areas of our country experiencing rapid population growth, Smart Growth measures alone cannot do the job. In these areas, Smart Growth measures must be augmented with efforts to rein in our mushrooming population.

To see that this is so, let's look at a way to forecast future open space losses, using a very simple formula. Agricultural land and large forested areas at the edge of a metropolitan area are obvious examples of what is meant by open space. The term also encompasses undeveloped land within a metropolitan area: agricultural lands, parks, and park-like areas – virtually any green spaces that connect the residents with nature. In other words open space is simply the total land area in a region of interest minus the developed land area in that region. Consequently, the amount of open space that vanishes over an interval of time is equal to the increase in developed land over the same interval of time.[17]

At any point in time the amount of developed land area in a region is determined by two factors: per capita land use and the population. More specifically, the amount of developed land, A, in an urban area is equal to the population, P, of that area times the per capita land use, U, i.e.,

$$A = P \times U.$$

For example, if the population consists of one thousand people and the per capita land consumption is 0.25 acres, then the developed land area will be 250 acres.

Using the $A = P \times U$ formula we can observe how the amount of developed land changes when either of the two factors change. For example, if the population remains at 1,000 but the per capita land consumption grows by 50% (to 0.375 acres), then the developed land also grows by 50%, from 250 to 375 acres. On the other hand, if the per capita land use remains

Growth Pains 11

constant at 0.25 acres but the population grows by 50% (to 1,500 people), the developed land grows the same amount, i.e., from 250 to 375 acres.

In both cases 125 acres of previously undeveloped land is lost to development, i.e., in both cases 125 acres of open space vanish. Hence we see clearly that vanishing open space can be caused by increases in either population or per capita land use.

Not surprisingly, an increase in developed land is seldom due to either increasing population or increasing per capita land consumption acting alone, but both factors acting simultaneously. Estimates provided in a recent Brookings Institution report indicate that developed land in the Washington area jumped 47% between 1982 and 1997.[18] Moreover, when the data in the report is applied to the "A = P x U" formula, it can be readily determined that at least 63% of this huge loss of open space was due to population growth.[19] This means that for every acre of Washington area land lost to increasing per capita land consumption, about two acres were lost due to our rapid population growth.

Another report, one addressing sprawl over a different period, indicates that developed land in the Washington area nearly doubled between 1970 and 1990, and that 47% of this increase was due to population growth.[20]

The conclusion to be drawn is obvious. If we are to keep our open spaces from vanishing, we must acknowledge the role of our mushrooming population.

Let's look now at the implications for the future of the Washington region.

The next 25 years. Between 1982 and 1997 per capita land consumption in the Washington urban area grew by 13%. Let us consider an optimistic scenario and suppose that over the next 25 years, Smart Growth policies will be able to completely stop per capita land consumption growth. That is, let us suppose that the per capita land consumption remains at about the 1997 level. Under this scenario the lost open space over the next 25 years would be due solely to population growth.

The projected population growth for the extended Washington area is 1.6 million over the next 25 years.[21] Using this number in conjunction with the 1997 per capita land consumption of 0.17 acres,[22] we can project that the amount of vanishing open space would be 425 square miles. This is clearly a huge open space loss, but to help grasp its true enormity, note that it is the equivalent of taking metropolitan Denver (as of 1990) and dropping it down on Washington area open space![23]

The longer term. It is obvious from the preceding that just stopping the growth in per capita land consumption will not arrest our enormous open space losses. Therefore let us postulate that over the next 25 years, aggressive Smart Growth policies could dramatically reduce per capita land consumption in the Washington region. In particular, let us suppose that over the next 25 years we could reduce the per capita consumption to 0.125 acres.

Figure 2-1 compares the projected growth in Washington urbanized area over the years 2025 to 2100 using two per capita land use assumptions: the 1997 per capita land use of 0.17 acres and the more optimistic 0.125 acres per person. In examining the figure we note that, regardless of the per capita land consumption assumed, the lost open space steadily increases. This is so because Washington area population has steadily increased in the past and is projected to do so in the future (as we shall see later in this report).

We also see from Figure 2-1 that, for any given year, the urbanized area with the lower per capita land use is substantially less. For example, the difference in 2025 is about 480 square miles. If in the next 23 years we could save such an

Growth Pains

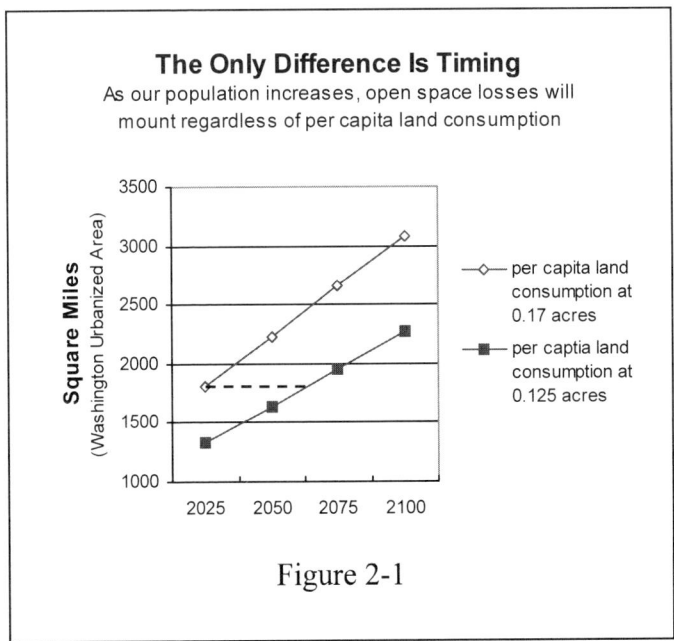

Figure 2-1

enormous amount of open space from development, we would all have cause for celebrating. Or would we?

The fact is that the land "saved" would be lost in a little over a generation as a result of the projected Washington area population growth. (We can see this by noting the horizontal dashed line in Figure 2-1.) Consequently the only thing that we could honestly celebrate is delaying the loss of the 480 square miles by about 37 years.

Figure 2-1 clearly shows us that any benefit from achieving a lower per capita land consumption is only temporary if our population continues to grow. With a growing population there is always some time in the future at which open space losses associated with more frugal per capita land use catches up with the lost open space resulting earlier from more extravagant per capita land use. Even if we are able to substantially reduce per capita land use, continued massive population growth will result in continued massive open space losses.

Increasing density is a tool, not a solution. A per capita land consumption of 0.125 acres corresponds to a density of 8 persons per urbanized acre. In 1997, Metropolitan Washington had a density of 5.88 persons per urbanized acre and ranked as the 17th most densely populated metropolitan area.[24] Achieving a density of 8 persons per acre would mean nearly matching the density of the most densely populated metropolitan area in the continental Untied States: Los Angeles-Anaheim-Riverside, CA.[25]

Personal preferences weigh heavily on what is considered an acceptable density, and many people recoil at the thought of living in an area as crowded as Los Angeles. But there are also many people who would agree that a density of 8 persons per acre can provide a variety of pleasant living accommodations. By way of illustration, consider the community of Montgomery Village in Montgomery County, MD – 1990 density of 7.7 persons per acre. The Village is a community of about 32,000 people living in a mixture of single family homes on modest lots, town homes, and mid-rise apartments. The community enjoys a network of biker/hiker paths, multiple man-made lakes, and ample outdoor recreational space including dozens of tennis courts, ball fields, and a golf course. The community also enjoys schools that are in walking distance and retail facilities that are in walking distance for many. In short, this community embodies much of the American Dream while still being more land use efficient than most places in Maryland.

On the other hand, it is obvious that if we increase density well over 8 persons per acre, it will not be possible to offer the housing choices and community amenities offered by Montgomery Village, or the many similar communities in the area. Increasing urban densities is a rational response to run away population growth. But there are limits.

Recall that Oregon's famed Urban Growth Boundaries expand with increasing population. They do so because there is a limit to the density that people will accept; there is a limit to how quickly density changes can be implemented. Given such limits, we know with mathematical certainty that unless we address population growth as well as per capita land consumption, our open space will continue to vanish with astonishing rapidity.

Relying solely on high density urban development is a deeply flawed open space preservation strategy. Worse, it is a strategy that could diminish our children's appreciation of the natural world:

"Most kids don't have the opportunity to experience the outdoors firsthand. For them, nature is something they get secondhand. Virtual nature. And this is a problem. ... can kids get passionate about something that's never been a real part of their lives?"

Matt Hamilton, high school student,
Sixth Annual Environmental Summit,
Annapolis Maryland, January 17, 2000

Road Congestion

While a great many people lament the loss of open space caused by sprawl, nothing rouses passions like road congestion. In late 2000, fully 75% of Prince George's and Montgomery County residents indicated that traffic congestion is a major problem.[26]

Our congestion, an irritant since the late-sixties, has unquestionably become much worse. The problem is that there are too many vehicles on our roads. Or as members of the Growth Machine would phrase it, our roads have not kept pace with our vehicles.

Growth Machine spokespersons and the media often exclaim that the Washington area congestion is the 2nd worst in the country (or the 3rd or 4th worst, depending on the particular study outcome being cited). Such exclamations never mention how close the competition is. We should not be fooled into thinking that our area is suffering disproportionately, and that we need to demand that the inequity be remedied. The fact is that all who live in large metropolitan areas are essentially in the same increasingly objectionable situation (Figure 2-2).[27]

The prognosis for the Washington area is that congestion will get worse than it is now. As we shall see, the primary reason is population growth.

Why is our congestion worse? A vehicle that travels ten miles contributes ten VMT (vehicle miles traveled) to the traffic statistics of an area. At the area-wide level, traffic engineers measure the traffic load on a road system as the ratio of VMT per day to Lane-Miles of road. This ratio simply allows engineers to quantify what is obvious to all of us: the more cars on our roads and the greater distances that they travel, the worse our congestion is going to be.

Growth Pains

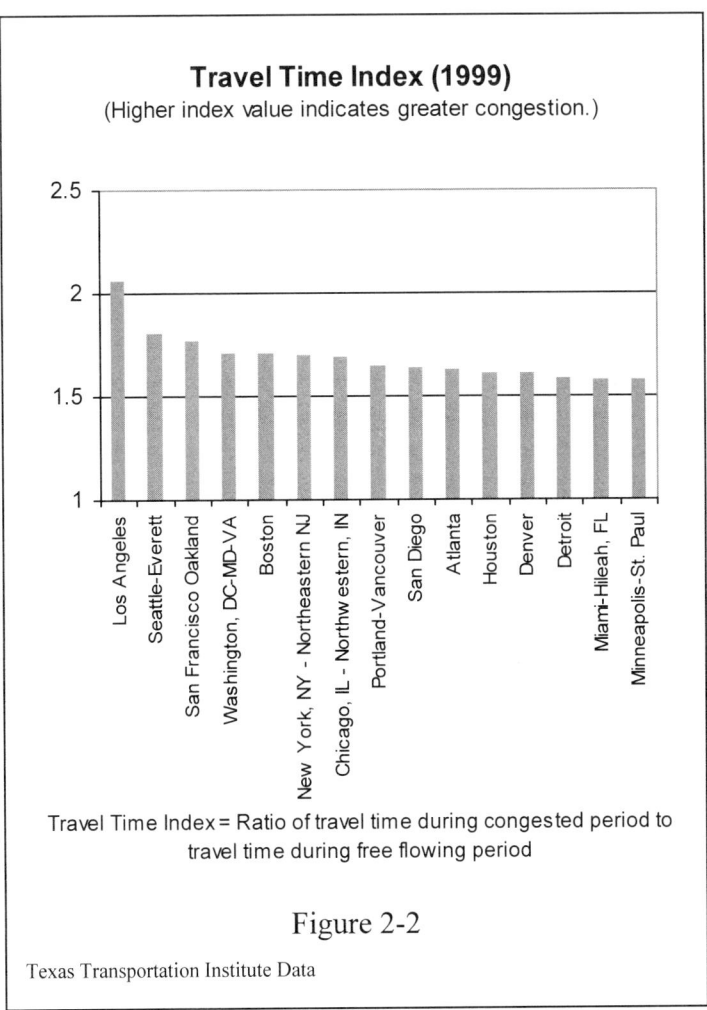

Figure 2-2

Texas Transportation Institute Data

According to the Texas Transportation Institute (TTI, at Texas A&M University), the traffic load on Washington area freeways and Principal Arterial Streets (PAS) has increased significantly. From 1982 to 1999, TTI estimates that the load (per lane-mile of road) on our Principal Arterial Streets increased 16%, and the load on our freeways increased a whopping 47%.[28] Given that the area was already congested in 1982, there is little wonder that area residents increasingly complain.

It would be wrong to conclude from our worsening congestion that the Washington area authorities have not been building roads. According to the TTI, more than a thousand lane-miles of roads were built between 1982 and 1999 – enough freeway alone to reach from D.C. to Chicago (600 miles). Yet our congestion became worse. The reason: our VMT growth exceeded our road growth.

To understand why our area VMT is growing so rapidly, let's consider the key influencing factors. The VMT for an area is the sum of all the miles driven per day by the people traveling in that area. This sum can be expressed as the product of the population of the area and the average daily miles traveled per person:

$$VMT = Population \times Per\ Capita\ VMT$$

If the population increases but the per capita VMT remains fixed, then the VMT will increase in proportion to the population increase. If per capita VMT increases but the population remains fixed, the VMT will increase in proportion to the per capita VMT increase. If both population and per capita VMT increase, then both factors obviously contribute to the increase in VMT.

Figure 2-3 depicts these increases using TTI data for the period 1982 to 1999.[29] Clearly, increases in population *and* per capita VMT were both major contributors to the area VMT growth over this period. Figure 2-4 indicates the projected increases for the period 2000 to 2025 based on data from the Metropolitan Washington Council of Governments (COG).[30] For the first quarter of the new century, growth in per capita VMT is expected to contribute relatively little to the area VMT growth. If COG's projections withstand the test of time, the bulk of our future VMT growth will be due to population growth.[31]

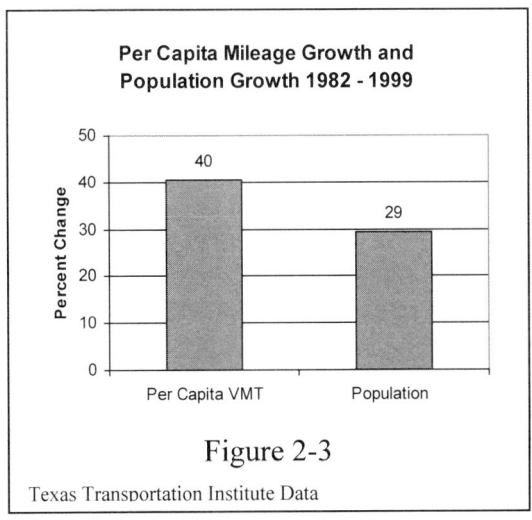

Figure 2-3
Texas Transportation Institute Data

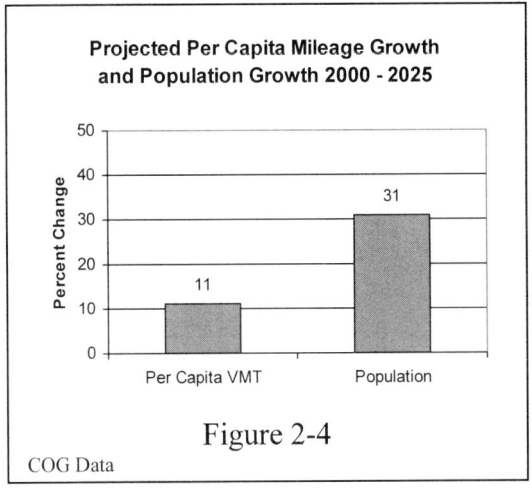

Figure 2-4
COG Data

Just build more roads? Naturally, the Growth Machine urges that we build roads in proportion to the increase in VMT.

But with relatively few exceptions this is happening nowhere in the country. According to the TTI, the Washington area and nearly all major areas over the country have opted not to build roads in proportion to VMT. Consequently the VMT load has increased relative to lane-miles of roadway available to carry the load. In turn the road congestion has worsened not just in the Washington area, but all over the country (Figure 2-5).[32]

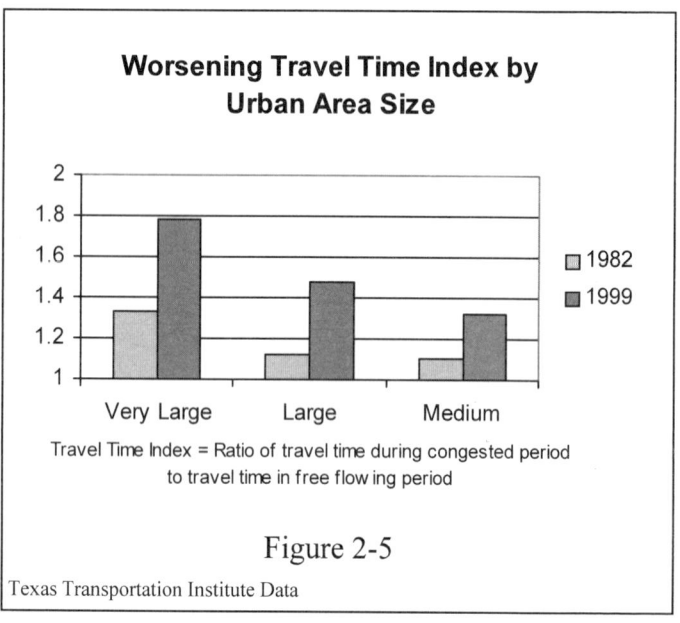

Figure 2-5

Texas Transportation Institute Data

Given that failing to grow roadway capacity at the same rate as VMT causes congestion to increase, why has most of the country elected greater congestion rather than attempting to grow roads as fast as VMT?

Of course, cost is one reason. A commission appointed by Maryland's Governor Glendening has warned that the state must spend at least $27 billion more than planned over the next two decades to prevent traffic from growing significantly worse. And according to officials, traffic jams will still be inevitable even with this huge increase.[33]

But in addition to cost, an equally important reason is the damage to the communities through which the roads would be built. According to the TTI, "The need for new roads exceeds the funding capacity *and the ability to gain environmental and public approval.* The answer to the question 'Can more roads solve all of the problem?' doesn't lie in esoteric or theoretical discussions as [much as] in practical limitations. In many of the nation's most congested corridors there doesn't seem to be the space, money and public approval to add enough road space to create an acceptable condition."[34]

As an urban area expands, the more congested roads are not at the periphery where the new communities are sprouting up, but in the established suburbs through which those in the outer suburbs commute. For a variety of reasons the land which was set aside for expansion of roadways in the established suburbs cannot meet the growing demand for expansion. Consequently increasing the lane-miles of road where the congestion is greatest means taking private property and/or public park land, increasing noise and pollution, and decreasing property values. In turn this leads to resistance from the citizens of the area where the land is being taken.

Elected politicians see this resistance as a potential political cost. Resistance from a small group may be regarded as a nuisance, but widespread resistance is taken more seriously. An illustration of this involves the Techway (a proposed road and bridge connecting Dulles, VA with Gaithersburg, MD) and Representative Frank Wolf of Virginia. Mr. Wolf, initially a strong proponent of the Techway, reversed his position after an outcry from citizens on both sides of the Potomac. In a letter to the *Washington Post* Mr. Wolf explained his reversal in terms of the extensive adverse impact the road and bridge would have on neighborhoods, parklands, and wetlands.[35]

The developers and the citizens who will benefit from a specific road expansion, often refer disparagingly to those who resist the road coming through their neighborhoods as NIMBYs (Not In My Back Yard). But this characterization fails to recognize that the residents of the established suburbs are often asked to sacrifice quality of life in their community to serve the needs of the developers, land speculators, and the people moving to the outer suburbs. In other words, road building in established communities is not a win-win enterprise. It is at best a win-lose enterprise, and the potential losers can be expected to fight to keep their community from being adversely affected.

If our regional population were stable, new roads could be planned and built in a way that would provide more effective relief, and road planners could at least assure adversely affected communities that their sacrifice would not be in vain. But with our mushrooming population, new roads quickly become saturated with traffic – particularly in our major transportation corridors.

Major transportation corridors in the Washington area include I-95 to the south of the city, and I-270 to the north. Both of these interstates have been widened within the last decade or so. The widening initially brought much needed relief, but the congestion returned in an astonishingly short period of time.[36]

In 1999, just eight years after completion, traffic load on the widened I-270 had already exceeded what the planners had projected for the year 2010. How could a major road expansion that required 17 years for planning and construction become congested in only eight years? A consultant was hired by local officials to address this question. After analyzing the available data, he concluded that unexpectedly high growth in jobs and population caused the road to become re-congested so quickly.[37]

Just build more roads? As we add more than 0.5 million people to the Washington area with each passing decade, we have no choice but to build more roads. But in the face of a population mushrooming into the indefinite future, building more roads is not a solution to our traffic congestion. It is an exercise in swimming against a narrowly overwhelming current: there may be moments when we seem to make progress, but overall we are moving backward.

What about telecommuting? Commentary about our congestion typically focuses on commuting to and from work, and telecommuting is often hailed as our salvation. Telecommuting is an excellent idea, but it will not provide major relief for two reasons.

First, commuting accounts for a surprisingly modest fraction of our driving. Nationally, commuting to work accounts for 24% of our vehicle trips and 31% of our Vehicle Miles Traveled (VMT).[38] This leaves 76% of our trips and 69% of our local travel distances for shopping, family/personal business, recreation and social visiting, and travel to schools and churches.

Second, our mushrooming population diminishes the effectiveness of telecommuting. If our regional population were stable, widespread telecommuting would have a lasting impact on our rush hour congestion. But with a rapidly growing population, any decrease in the number of work trips due to acceptance of telecommuting will be offset soon by the increase in the number of work trips due to our population growth (Figure 2-6). Telecommuting can make our situation better, but it cannot keep it from getting worse year by year.

What about Metrorail? The Washington area is privileged to have one of the most modern subway systems in the country. Nearly all Washington area residents have benefited from Metrorail, and expansion of the Metrorail system is a critically important part of our future. However, there are no silver bullets: an expanded Metro system will lessen the impact of population growth on Washington area quality of life, but it will not cure our mobility ills.

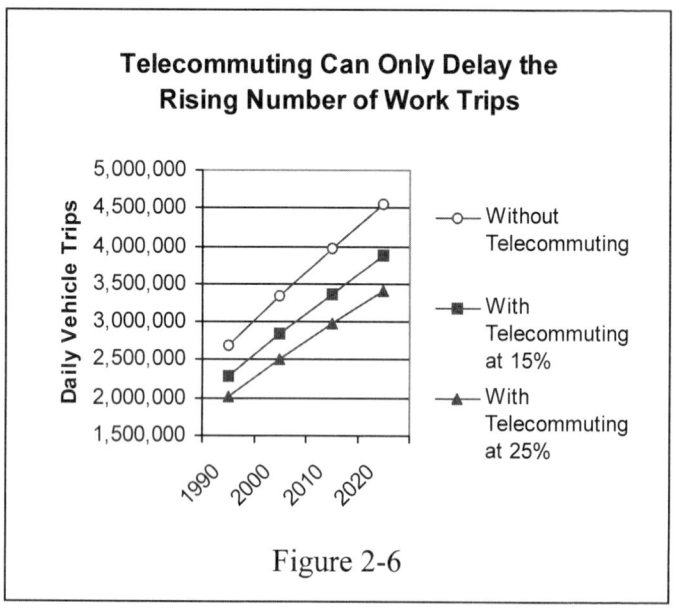

Figure 2-6

Metrorail construction began in 1969, and operation has been incrementally expanded as the various segments were completed. The full system was only recently completed; so it is somewhat surprising to learn that the current ridership (about 650,000 trips per day[39]) is already beginning to stress the capacity of the system. According to Metro General Manager Richard A. White, "The Red and Orange lines are close to capacity now," and his agency is studying Metro capacity and trying to determine when it will reach its limits.[40]

In contrast to the 650,000 Metrorail trips per day, the current number of vehicle trips per day in the WMA is 15.6 million. Worse, the number of daily vehicle trips is projected to increase by nearly 5.5 million over the next twenty years.[41] Over the next twenty five years WMATA plans to expand Metro's rail-miles by 50% (50 – 60 miles) and install numerous station improvements to the existing line.[42] But even if these improvements result in a doubled Metrorail ridership, the increased ridership would be only 12% of the projected vehicle trip *growth*. This statistic rather dramatically teaches us two things. First, the planned Metrorail expansion will be desperately needed if our population grows as projected, and second, even a 100% increase in ridership cannot do more than make a modest dent in the traffic caused by the projected population growth.

Beyond cost, perhaps the most vexing problem associated with extensively expanding Metro is the enormous size of the WMA and the trend toward suburb-to-suburb travel. The land area of the counties comprising the Washington Metropolitan Statistical Area is 3,931 square miles (4,599 square miles for the Extended Washington Area).[43] The vast majority of this area is several miles from the nearest metro station. Almost all of the 83 Metro stations are located inside the beltway, and the area inside the beltway comprises less than 10% of the total WMA land area. Figure 2-7 illustrates this overwhelming scale of the Washington area in comparison to Metrorail extensions outside the beltway (the black dots).[44] Clearly, the existing Metrorail system is simply not applicable to a great portion of the trip needs.

The inapplicability of Metrorail to the bulk of future trips is even more sobering. Projections indicate that as early as 2010, nearly 50% of daily to/from work person trips in the WMA will be suburb-to-suburb.[45] A primary force behind the trend toward suburb-to-suburb travel is office space located in the suburbs. According to the Brookings Institution nearly 59% of commercial office space in the Washington area is located in the suburbs. And of that 59%, less than half is concentrated in edge cites such as Tysons Corner. The majority is scattered around the suburbs in tiny disconnected pockets.[46]

A Metrorail expansion designed to serve a major portion of suburb-to-suburb travel is difficult to imagine when both businesses and residences are sprinkled over 4,000 square miles. Most people will use Metrorail only if at least one end

Metrorail stations are miles from where most area residents live and work.

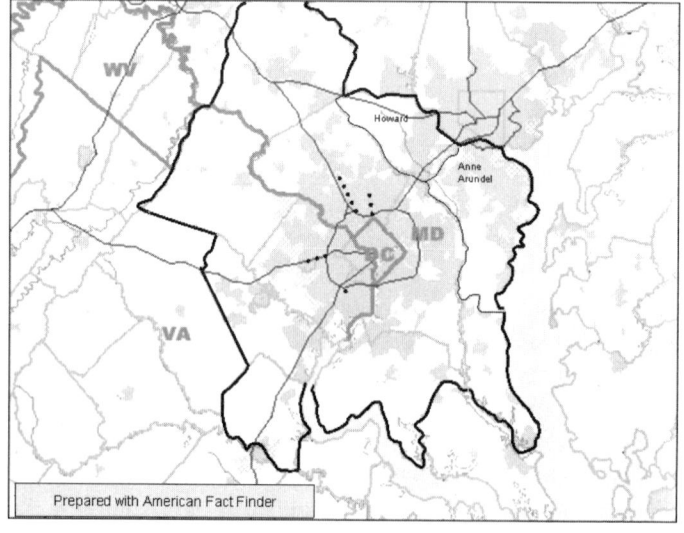

Figure 2-7

The heavy dark line circumscribes the counties of the Extended Washington Area. The shaded areas identify Census Bureau defined *1990* urban areas in the Baltimore-Washington region. The black dots indicate MetroRail extensions beyond the beltway.

of a trip is within walking distance of a Metro station. Consequently a viable suburb-to-suburb rail system is possible only if suburban development is concentrated at edge cities ("regional activity centers" in COG terminology) such as Tysons Corner, VA.

Unfortunately, business and residences of the Extended Washington Area are already spread out over an area 15 times the size of the area circumscribed by the beltway. Moreover, the evidence shows that business in suburbia is not accreting around a few major growth poles, but disperses throughout the metropolitan area. Ironically, one reason for this is that edge

Growth Pains

cities face the same land cost and vehicle congestion pressures as the central cities.[47]

So, what about Metrorail? The current system is nearing capacity, and expanding the system is an obvious high-priority need. Yet, even if all 150 miles of *potential* rail expansions identified in WMATA's 1999 plan were constructed, Metrorail would still serve only a small fraction of our 4,000 square mile area.[48] And even if ridership on an expanded Metrorail doubles or triples, just the *growth* in vehicular trips over the next twenty years will be far greater than the *total* Metrorail ridership. Metrorail simply cannot cure our mobility ills – particularly if we allow our population to grow as projected.

What's the bottom line? In a large, colorful brochure, titled "Making the VISION a Reality…TOGETHER," the Metropolitan Washington Council of Governments (COG) invites the public to "Help us plan a *better* transportation future for the Washington Region." In glancing at this brochure most would infer that we can look forward to a transportation system that is better in 2020 than it is today. But this is not the case.

In developing its recent report, the Montgomery County Transportation Policy Task Force used a computer model to predict future travel demand based on different scenarios, including one with "significant roadway component" and one with "significant rail transit component." The model predicts that over the next 25 years, the percentage of congested lane miles will increase markedly, from 7.1 percent in 1998 to 10-12 percent in 2025, regardless of which scenario (road or transit) is elected. And by 2050 the percentage is projected to increase to nearly 16 percent regardless of scenario.[49] While the task force model focused on Montgomery County, the results are emblematic of the regional future. With lane-miles of road expanding only 13% while population and VMT expand 31% and 46% respectively, greater congestion throughout the Washington area is inevitable.[50]

The prognosis for the Washington area is that congestion will get worse than it is now. The primary reason is population growth. The projected increase in the number of vehicles alone is a staggering 1.6 million in just 20 years.[51] If we were to line these vehicles up, bumper to bumper, they would stretch from Washington to San Francisco, *and back again*. While planning agencies portray the future through rose colored glasses, and local politicians promote continued mushrooming growth, we can expect only worsening congestion. The number of vehicles, the number of households, the number of jobs, are simply growing beyond the limits of realistic transportation system improvements.

The Willamette Valley in Oregon is also bracing for worsening traffic.

"How's the traffic out there? A nightmare or not too bad? Whatever the traffic is like today in your neck of the Willamette Valley, planners say it's likely to be worse tomorrow, and in ten years, and in 50 years."

"The future is in our hands,"
The Willamette Chronicle, April 2001.

Water Worries

In 1999 in Poolesville, a town in northwestern Montgomery County which gets its water from a municipal well, concern over the depleted water table prompted some residents to argue that further development should be restricted. That same year in Boyds, in central Montgomery County, residents concerned about their water table organized to oppose a proposed golf course. Their concern: the water used to keep the fairways green would make their wells run dry.[52]

Historically, the Washington area water supply has greatly exceeded the demand, and the people of the Washington area have taken their water for granted. But as the area population has mushroomed, the demand for water has risen, drought related shortages have been experienced, and conflicts have begun to emerge. According to Jim Gerhart of the Baltimore office of the U.S. Geological Survey: "The more growth, the more conflict. And the drought doesn't help."[53]

Washington area water worries started in the late 70s with a serious drought and mandatory water restrictions. Serious water worries surfaced again in 1999 when the entire state of Maryland was placed under mandatory water restrictions.[54] And as of the spring of 2002, portions of the Washington area are once again under water use restrictions.

People in the Metropolitan area who depend on well water are the most vulnerable to drought. Their concern is literally running dry. U.S. Geological Survey figures released April 5, 2002 show that ground-water levels across Maryland set record lows for March. Eight of the 17 wells monitored by the USGS were lower than ever before in March. On the same day, Maryland's Governor Glendening imposed mandatory water restrictions in areas dependent on well water, including Frederick County and parts of Montgomery and Howard Counties. "No one should take false hope and say, 'Gee, we just had rain,'" Glendening said. "We are in serious trouble."[55]

Shortly after imposition of these latest restrictions, in an article in the *Washington Post*, the former director of the EPA's Chesapeake Bay Program (Bill Matuszeski) recommended three steps to reduce our vulnerability to future droughts. His first priority: "local and state growth policies should actively discourage building of new homes that rely on private wells."[56] Though possibly not his intent, his recommendation clearly makes the connection between population growth and our water worries. In effect he is acknowledging that our population growth is exceeding our ground water resources. His recommendation, on the other hand, tacitly assumes that surface water resources will always be adequate to our population. But as we shall see, water worries are not limited to those dependent on wells.

The Washington Metropolitan Area obtains about 75% of its water from the Potomac River.[57] Our average collective daily demand (D) for Potomac water is driven by two factors, population (P) and per capita daily water consumption (WC), i.e.:

$$D = P \times WC.$$

As the population of the Washington area has grown, the amount of water withdrawn from the Potomac has steadily increased. Smart Growth has little impact on the increasing demand. According to the Interstate Commission for the Potomac River Basin, people who live in multi-family dwelling units consume less water, on average, than those who live in single family units – but not substantially less.[58] This means that the value for WC in the above equation will change little as a consequence of the type of future Washington area development. Regardless of the mix of high density and low density development, our future demand for water will just keep climbing in proportion to Washington area population growth.

Growth Pains

Figure 2-8 indicates projected growth in average daily demand (the inclined line) in relation to flows during two record drought periods.[59, 60]

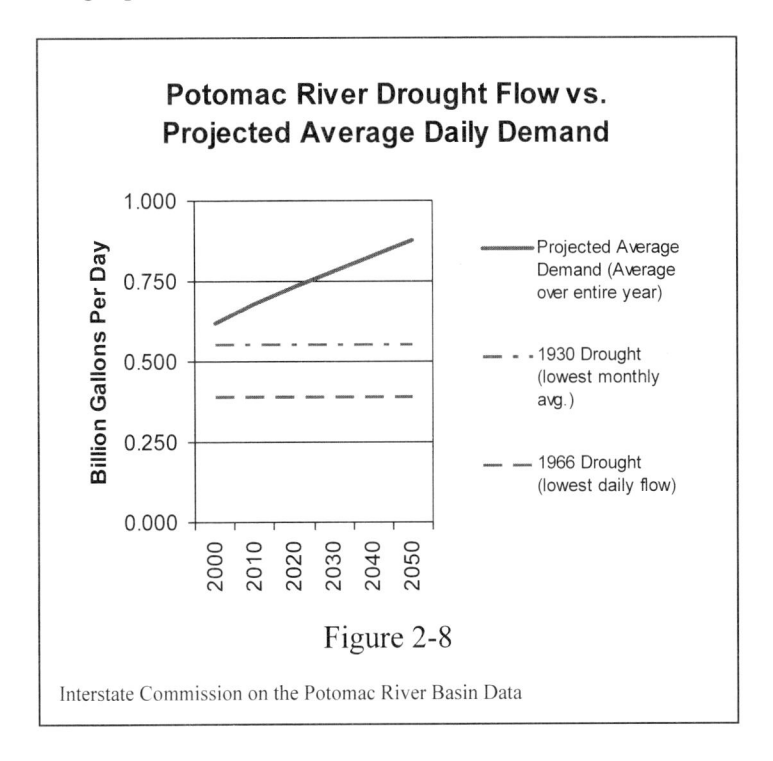

Potomac River Drought Flow vs. Projected Average Daily Demand

[Graph showing Billion Gallons Per Day (0.000 to 1.000) on y-axis and years 2000 to 2050 on x-axis, with three lines:
— Projected Average Demand (Average over entire year)
– – – 1930 Drought (lowest monthly avg.)
– – 1966 Drought (lowest daily flow)]

Figure 2-8

Interstate Commission on the Potomac River Basin Data

Drought year data presented in Figure 2-8 includes both the worst month (1930) and the worst day (1966). As suggested by the 1966 worst day flow, the flow on any given day of a drought can be substantially lower than the drought's monthly average. Hence, even when the monthly average drought flow exceeds our daily demand, it is likely that on one or more days the daily flow will be below the daily demand.

Even in periods of relatively mild droughts (like the 1999 drought), Potomac River flow can fall below the amount that we use. In order to minimize the likelihood of water rationing during droughts, water is stored in reservoirs to provide an additional source. The capacity of these reservoirs is adequate for our present needs, but before today's toddlers become adults, the capacity of these reservoirs will cease to meet the needs of our growing demand.

Potomac Reservoir Origins

In the 1950s, officials first began to be concerned that projected population growth in the region would eventually lead to a demand for water in excess of available supply.[61] A number of potential measures for increasing supply were studied at that time – including reservoirs.

The Corps of Engineers conducted a study that identified 16 potential dam sites on the Potomac upstream of Washington, D.C. whose reservoirs could augment water supply during low flow periods.[62] There was significant public opposition to many of these sites. Only one, Jennings Randolph Reservoir near Bloomington, Md., was ever built. It was completed in 1982.[63] In 1984, the Little Seneca Reservoir was built a few miles from the Potomac in Black Hills Park in Montgomery County, Md.

For any given demand, the adequacy of the reservoirs depends on the severity of the drought and its duration. To reduce the probability of depleting the reservoirs before the end of a drought, conservation rules have been established. When the combined water volume falls to 60% of capacity, local governments are to urge citizens to voluntarily conserve water. When the water volume of either reservoir falls to 25% of capacity, local governments are to initiate mandatory water use restrictions.[64]

Looking at the population growth projected for the next fifty years it has become apparent that a severe drought occurring sometime after 2020 will result in the Jennings Randolph and Little Seneca reservoirs being inadequate.[65] Consequently, additional reservoirs or other means will have to be undertaken to assure an adequate water supply for the Washington area.

More Reservoirs?

If additional reservoirs are to be constructed, they will probably be built on a site previously identified and rejected. The largest of the sites identified in the past is in Seneca, Maryland. This would be a major impoundment on the mainstem of the Potomac adjacent to Loudoun, Montgomery, and Frederick Counties. The effects of construction of this dam would be so great, including flooding of the Chesapeake and Ohio National Historic Park and innumerable private properties, that it seems an unlikely option.[66]

All of the other sites encompass agricultural areas, or lie along streams in areas that are highly valued for their scenic and aesthetic qualities and are bordered by low to moderate density residential development.

Because of their impact on recreational land and cropland, new reservoirs will meet strong resistance from the communities of people (local and far flung) who will lose access to treasured natural or agricultural areas. As our growing population makes increasing demands on limited outdoor recreational space, the scenic, aesthetic, and recreational values of free flowing streams are increasingly seen as important. Indeed, a 1983 U.S. Army Corps of Engineers report makes it clear that opinion about reservoirs has declined drastically since 1963.[67]

Recycling Our Wastewater?

Since public opposition to more reservoirs may make them politically impractical, other options must be examined. One option is to pump the wastewater from the Blue Plains (D.C.) sewage treatment plant back up-river to the intake of the Washington Aqueduct. This approach could significantly reduce the Washington Aqueduct's need to withdraw "natural" water from the Potomac, in essence allowing Washington Aqueduct customers to keep reusing the same water.[68]

The major concern about this strategy clearly relates to its health implications: whether the Blue Plains discharge would be sufficiently cleansed to protect the public health. The idea of recycling Blue Plains effluent was tested at the Potomac Estuary Experimental Water Treatment Plant (EWTP), constructed and operated at Blue Plains between 1980 and 1983. During this time the EWTP tested a number of different treatment processes, and two were found to produce water of acceptable quality to be used as raw water.[69]

While the EWTP results look promising, it is difficult to be sanguine about recycling wastewater. The concern is not bacteria, but chemicals. We are often said to live in the information age, but it could just as easily be said that we live in the chemical age. Between 1940 and 1982, production of synthetic materials increased 350 times. In 1992 U.S. production of carbon-based synthetic chemicals topped 435 billion pounds, or 1,600 pounds per capita. Around the world, approximately one hundred thousand synthetic chemicals are on the market, and each year about one thousand new substances are introduced, most of them without adequate testing or review.[70]

In March of 2002, the *Washington Post* reported that the first nationwide study of pharmaceutical pollution of rivers and streams offers an unsettling picture of waterways contaminated with antibiotics, steroids, synthetic hormones and other commonly used drugs. Of the 139 streams analyzed by the U.S. Geological Survey in 30 states – including Maryland and Virginia – about 80 percent contained trace amounts of contaminants that are routinely discharged into the water via human and livestock waste and chemical plant refuse. Many of the chemical compounds detected are not covered by drinking-water standards or government health advisories, and little is known about how the interaction of those chemicals can affect humans, animals, and the environment.[71]

Growth Pains

About twelve years ago anglers fishing in English rivers reported that something strange was happening to the fish, particularly in the lagoons just below the discharge from sewage treatment plants. The problem was not the usual fish kills or obvious disease. But many of the fish looked quite bizarre – they showed both male and female sexual characteristics. Hormone mimics were suspected immediately, and tests soon confirmed the suspicion.

The source of the mimics was the subject of much investigation. At first researchers theorized that women taking oral contraceptives were excreting a synthetic estrogen in their urine, and that the synthetic was passing through the treatment plants and into the rivers. But this chemical was never detected in water released from the treatment plants.

Ultimately the researchers focused on a surprising candidate: soap detergent. They were not able to pin point detergents as the cause, but strongly suspected that detergent breakdown products (alkylphenols), perhaps in combination with pesticides and plasticizers, were the cause.[72]

The presence of such a biologically active mimic obviously raises questions about human consumption – particularly by pregnant women. The human embryo can be devastatingly affected by chemicals that confuse the developmental process. Few people in America have not heard of the health tragedies stemming from previously unheard of chemicals such as Thalidomide or DES. Sometimes extremely small quantities of a chemical agent are enough to cause adverse consequences. As little as one part per *ten trillion* of free estrogen is capable of altering the course of development in the womb.[73] The point is not that known hormone mimics such as DES are of special concern; rather the point is that vanishingly small amounts of chemicals can spell big trouble for pregnant women.

Recycling of Blue Plains wastewater during a drought may be a reasonable risk and the best course of action if we do not curb our regional population growth. After all, sewage treatment plant effluents lie upstream of intakes to drinking water processing facilities in the Washington region today. For example, the Fairfax County Water Authority withdraws raw water from the Occoquan Reservoir downstream from the UOSA (Upper Occoquan Sewage Authority) treatment plant, treats it by conventional methods, and converts it into potable water delivered to over one million of its customers. This has been done with no apparent health problems, and without public opposition.[74]

On the other hand, whereas chemicals in the UOSA effluent are diluted by the Occoquan River before water is withdrawn from the reservoir, chemicals not removed at Blue Plains will be fed directly into the tap water treatment system during periods of recycling. The resulting increase in chemicals in the tap water will depend on the extent to which the Blue Plains facility can remove harmful chemicals, the extent to which water flowing "naturally" in the Potomac is added to the treated waste water, and the concentration of chemicals in the "naturally flowing" Potomac River. Unless the Blue Plains facility is very effective at removing chemicals, the increase in chemicals in the tap water may be dramatic.[75] When hazardous chemicals and drugs in our tap water increase to unprecedented levels, prudence will demand that pregnant women avoid drinking water from the tap.

Just a few decades ago the Potomac's natural flow provided all the water we needed – even during drought years. But as our population increases our children will experience both voluntary and mandatory water restrictions with increasing frequency, and they may ultimately be called upon to accept tap water with a host of chemical contaminates unknown today, and at concentrations that will be a nagging concern for many people.

Having to sacrifice lawns and gardens in times of drought, and having pregnant women rely on bottled water during severe droughts may not be serious impositions. But they are quality of life declines. And since average water consumption is pretty much the same in multi-family dwelling units and single family units, any water conservation resulting from Smart Growth will be overwhelmed by the increasing number of consumers. Smart Growth efforts cannot prevent our water worries from escalating with each generation. The only way to maintain our water related quality of life, is to stop ignoring the need to stabilize our population.

> More water devoted to human needs means less for sustenance of ecosystems, and in many areas nature is losing out fast.
>
> *South Florida's Everglades is buckling under pressure from pollution and water diversions to meet the demands of a rapidly growing population. According to the assistant superintendent of Everglades National Park, the stressed out system "could ecologically fail within the next 20 years."*
>
> Chapter 5, *Last Oasis*, by Sandra Postel,

Treasure the Chesapeake

"Fishermen call it the 'dead zone' — a barren patch in the Gulf of Mexico where their nets come up empty and their lines never record a strike. It moves around, waxes or wanes with the seasons, but always returns. In fact, the dead zone is growing — currently 7,728 square miles, an area the size of New Jersey that's void of baitfish, void of anything."[76]

From the early 1900s to the mid-80s, the health of our Chesapeake Bay declined at such a precipitous rate that a similar massive dead zone seemed to be its fate. But the prospect of turning what is historically one of the most productive estuaries in the world into an area devoid of life roused many people to action. A turning point was establishment of the Chesapeake Bay Agreement – the 1987 compact in which Maryland, Virginia, Pennsylvania, and the District of Columbia pledged to restore the Chesapeake. As a result of this agreement – in combination with the expenditure of millions of dollars and the work of thousands of people – the Bay's slide toward a dead zone has been arrested. On the other hand, this high profile effort is making only very slow progress toward returning the Bay to its former healthy and productive state.

How much has the compact actually achieved? "Not a lot," says Donald Boesch, president of the University of Maryland's Center for Environmental Science and a longtime Bay ecologist. "...even if our management practices have been successful, we don't see much of an impact yet. Pollution is down, but not as much as had been hoped. The bay's health doesn't seem to be rebounding as fast as expected. There are successes, but they're mixed: Rockfish are abundant, but they may not have enough food. Bay grasses are spreading, but they're disappearing in prime blue crab havens where they're needed most."[77]

Growth Pains

There are dozens of ways in which the health of the Bay is assessed: water clarity, dissolved oxygen levels, nitrogen and phosphorous levels, fish and crab stocks, etc. One of the better overall measures is the total acreage of Bay grasses (or submerged aquatic vegetation). Grasses are a good measure because they aren't under harvest pressure like crabs, oysters, and fish. In addition, they respond to improvements in water quality, which primarily occur through reductions in suspended sediment, phosphorus and nitrogen.[78]

At the signing of the original Chesapeake Bay Agreement, in 1987, the Bay's submerged aquatic vegetation had recovered from a low of less than 40,000 acres (in 1984) to about 50,000 acres. In 1993, the Chesapeake Bay Program set an interim goal of 114,000 acres to be reached by 2005.[79] Figure 2-9 shows what has been accomplished.[80] After an initial jump between 1987 and 1989, the progress has been glacial. Indeed, without the aid of the trendline in Figure 2-9, it is difficult to perceive any progress.

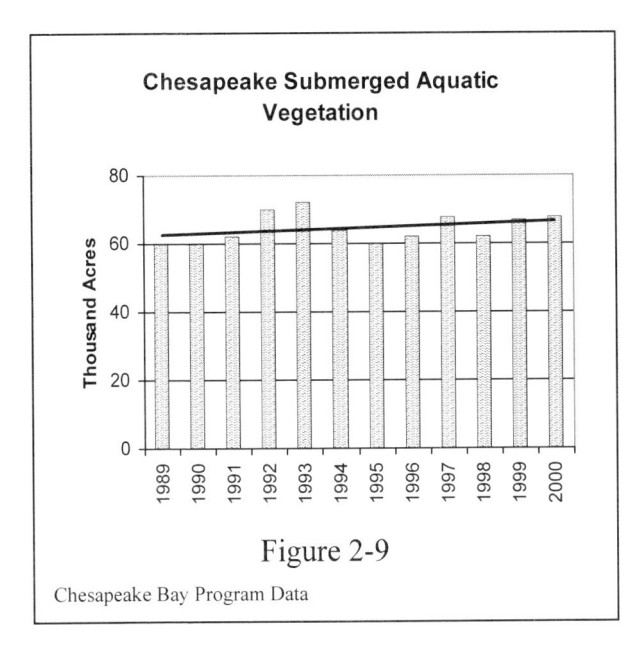

Figure 2-9

Chesapeake Bay Program Data

The trendline in Figure 2-9 depicts the best straight line fit to the data. The utility of the trendline is that it allows us to make a reasonable estimate of the trend in spite of the seemingly random year to year fluctuations. The equation (not shown) for this trendline indicates that the acreage of submerged aquatic vegetation is increasing at an average rate of only 374 acres per year.

We are still 45,000 acres short of the 114,000 acre goal. So we may conclude that, barring a significant improvement in the trend, the goal originally set for 2005 will not be achieved during the lifetime of anyone living today.

The effort to "cleanup" the Bay has involved federal, state, and local government agencies, high-profile non-governmental organizations such as the Chesapeake Bay Foundation, thousands of volunteers, and the expenditure of many millions of dollars. Yet noteworthy improvement, such as the recovery of the Striped Bass, has been spotty, and overall improvement has been very slow. Why?

A major reason is population growth in the Bay watershed. This growth has slowed the reduction of two of the pollutants most responsible for the decline of the Bay ecosystem: nitrogen and phosphorous. These pollutants are nutrients. In appropriate quantities they are essential to the Bay ecosystem. But in excessive quantities they cause algae blooms that rob the Bay of oxygen and prevent adequate sunlight from reaching the submerged aquatic vegetation. The result is an aquatic ecosystem that is stressed, and in the areas most affected an ecosystem that is severely stressed.

Let us consider a few examples in which population has impeded Bay restoration, and from these examples gain some insight into the probable future of the Chesapeake and those living within its watershed.

Growth Pains

Vehicle Nitrogen Oxide Emissions About 6% of the Bay nitrogen oxide load is the result of airborne nitrogen oxide falling directly to the water surface; an additional 21% of the Bay's nitrogen oxide load is due to airborne nitrogen oxide falling to land surface within the Bay watershed.[81] The significant sources of this airborne nitrogen oxide are emissions from vehicles and fossil fuel power plants.

Emission-control technology has greatly reduced the nitrogen oxide emission per vehicle mile traveled. As a result the annual nitrogen oxide emissions due to vehicles in the Bay watershed fell 18% between 1985 and 1997, while at the same time the vehicle miles traveled (VMT) increased by 41%.[82] Had the increase in VMT not occurred, vehicular nitrogen oxide emissions would have fallen 42% -- more than twice the actual decline.

Population growth can be blamed for a little less than half the vehicular nitrogen oxide reduction shortfall relative to the 42% reduction that could have been achieved. (As noted in the Road Congestion subchapter, population growth and per capita VMT growth were both major factors in our '82 – '99 VMT increase.) But future shortfalls will be largely due to population growth, since per capita VMT growth will play only a minor role in future VMT increases.

In a few decades the problem of vehicular nitrogen oxide emissions may be solved by technology. But over the intervening time there is a concern that the total vehicular nitrogen oxide emissions will reverse their downward trend. According to the Chesapeake Bay Program, VMT increases, fleet turnover and changes in fleet composition (such as the increasing popularity of less fuel efficient vehicles), and deterioration of emission-control equipment over time, may cause us to lose ground previously gained through improved vehicle emission-controls.[83]

Municipal Nitrogen Discharge. Nitrogen discharged from municipal sewage treatment plants declined 20% between 1985 and 2000, even though the watershed population increased 15% during that time.[84] Without the increase in population, the nitrogen discharged from municipal treatment plants would have decreased 30%.

The 20% decline was due to the introduction of nitrogen reduction technology (NRT) in a number of the municipal plants. As a result of continued upgrading of municipal plants with NRT, an additional 10% reduction in nitrogen discharged is anticipated by 2010. However, beyond 2010 the discharge from municipal plants may stop declining and begin to rise – reversing in part the gains achieved through the expenditure of millions of dollars. According to the Chesapeake Bay Program, "If no further actions are taken, we anticipate increased discharges after 2010 due to population growth."[85],[86]

Urban Runoff and Septic System Nitrogen. Lawn and garden fertilizers used in urban and suburban settings run off during heavy or protracted rain. The nitrogen from this runoff reaches the Bay through the streams in the watershed. Nitrogen from septic systems leaches into the groundwater and eventually makes its way to local waterways and the Bay.

There are efforts to educate the people living in the Chesapeake basin regarding runoff. But urban runoff of nitrogen is typically considered uncontrollable since it is the result of the habits and preferences of millions of people. And while there are nitrogen reduction technologies for septic systems, they are very expensive and unlikely to find wide application. Consequently, as the Chesapeake basin population continues to grow the nitrogen load from urban runoff and septic systems will continue to grow as well.

Between 1985 and 2000, these two sources of Bay nitrogen pollution were the only ones to increase. In 1985 the combined amount was 39 million pounds; in 2000 it was 49 million pounds.[87] This is a 25% increase in just 15 years, and it is primarily due to population growth.

It is instructive to compare the trends in nitrogen load due to point sources (primarily municipal sewage treatment plants) and the load due to urban runoff and septic systems (Figure 2-10). If we extrapolate the obvious trends, it is clear that a crossover is imminent. If our population continues to grow rapidly, in another fifteen years nitrogen from urban runoff and septic systems will be a greater problem than the nitrogen from point sources.

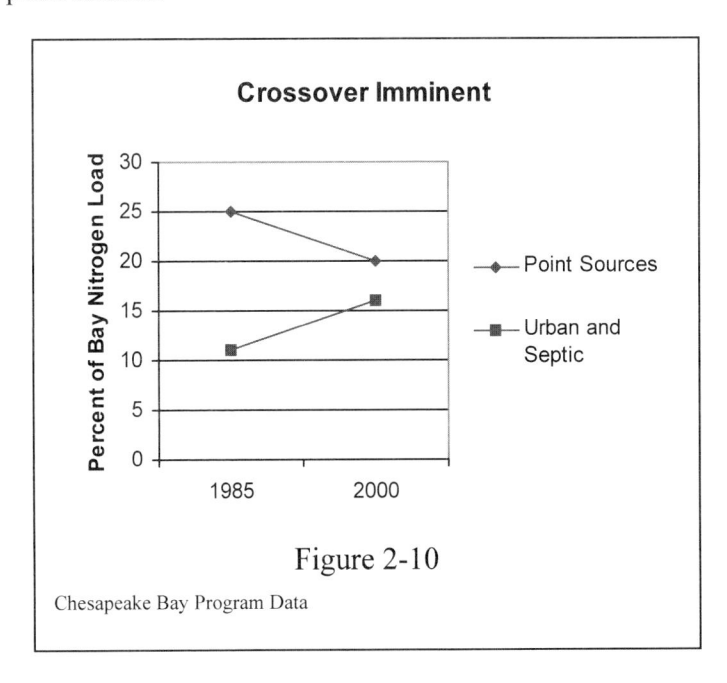

Crossover Imminent

[Graph showing Percent of Bay Nitrogen Load vs Year (1985, 2000). Point Sources decrease from 25 to 20. Urban and Septic increase from 11 to 16.]

Figure 2-10

Chesapeake Bay Program Data

Of course a trend is not a certain predictor of the future. Urban runoff will be less of a problem to the extent that Chesapeake watershed residents adopt lawn and garden practices that minimize nitrogen runoff. For example, use of slow release fertilizers and adopting landscape designs that rely less on grass and more on shrubs and groundcovers would be beneficial. Also, deciding to move into a townhouse or condominium rather than a single-family house will likely result in a lower per capita fertilizer use.

In other words, if we are to accommodate an ever increasing population and prevent urban runoff and septic system leaching from overwhelming our efforts to restore the Bay, we must change the way that we live. Or in the words of the Chesapeake Bay Foundation, "Without change [in the way that we live on the land], we cannot save the Bay."[88]

How much change are we willing to accept? Landscape design changes are relatively minor and may be accepted by most people. Changes involving a move to a higher density setting are far more significant and may be rejected by many people – particularly those with young families. No one can say how much change people will be willing to make, but it is clear that if our population continues to mushroom, ecological survival of the Bay will be increasingly subject to the amount of change people actually make.

At the top level there are only two approaches to restoring the Bay: the "accommodate population growth" approach and the "stabilize population" approach. There are strong voices for Bay preservation that speak only to the necessity for accommodating population growth. In the short run this may be the only viable tactic. After all, there is little we can do today to significantly reduce the population growth over the next five years. But when we take a longer view, a view that encompasses 25 to 100 years, it is clear that these voices are avoiding a critical part of the issue.

If we were to stabilize the Chesapeake watershed population within the next few years, our ability to preserve the Bay would cease to be a pressing question. With the preservation efforts already underway the future of the Bay would be secured without significant additional changes in the way we live.

Growth Pains

On the other hand, if we focus only on accommodating population growth, the population pressures will increase relentlessly with each passing decade. Preserving the Bay will be a never-ending battle.

Bay preservation organizations have done an outstanding job of publicizing the plight of the Bay and recruiting thousands of volunteers who gladly give their time, energy, and money to protect the Bay. But without grappling with the need to stabilize population in the watershed, it is unlikely that the Bay will ever be restored.

At the conclusion of the first Maryland and Virginia bi-state conference on the health of the Chesapeake Bay, the speaker chosen to summarize the conference ended his talk with the following:

"One theme has run like a thread through all the papers and discussions in this conference, ... It is an issue that is almost always evaded, and certainly never addressed seriously. Yet this is the root problem of the environment, the basic cause of all the other problems – the human population explosion... If we cannot cope with it, maybe everything else will be in vain."

Chapter 5, *Turning the Tide*, *Saving the Chesapeake Bay*
by Tom Horton and William Eichbaum
Island Press, 1991

3

Growth Pressures

"The problem of excessive population seems to be central to nearly every problem in our state."
George R. Ariyoshi, former Governor of Hawaii[89]

"If I had the power, I'd turn off the spigot and keep Oregon as it is today."
John Kitzhaber, Governor of Oregon[90]

While Smart Growth programs help to contain sprawl, such efforts alone are unable to stand against the population growth pressures that diminish our open space, the health of our treasured Chesapeake Bay, and our quality of life. Citizens, planners, and elected officials all need to understand how population growth works against sustaining a good quality of life. Part of this understanding involves a rudimentary knowledge of the rapidity with which our population has grown and is still growing.

Washington Area Population Growth

The Washington Metropolitan Statistical Area as defined by the U.S. Office of Management and Budget includes the District of Columbia, the following counties, and the independent cities within these counties:

<u>Maryland</u>	<u>Virginia</u>
Frederick	Loudoun
Montgomery	Arlington
Prince George's	Fairfax
Calvert	Prince William
Charles	Stafford

We will add to this list the Maryland counties of Anne Arundel and Howard, and call the resulting area the Extended Washington Area.[91]

According to the Metropolitan Washington Council of Governments (COG), the year 2000 population of the Extended Washington Area was 5.2 million people. Using COG data we can project the 2025 population of the Extended Washington Area to be 6.8 million.[92] This is an increase of 1.6 million people (31%) in just 25 years.

Figure 3-1 shows the population growth from 1950 to 2025. The trendline in Figure 3-1 – the straight line that best fits the data points – lets us see at a glance that the Extended Washington Area population has increased at a very steady rate over the past 50 years, and is expected to continue to do so for

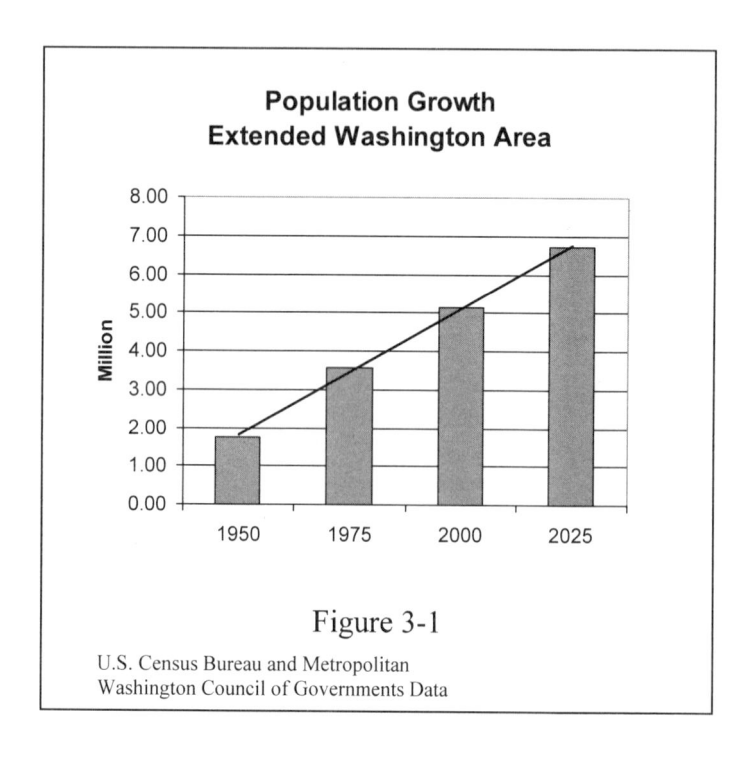

**Population Growth
Extended Washington Area**

Figure 3-1
U.S. Census Bureau and Metropolitan
Washington Council of Governments Data

at least the next 25 years. The rate of increase is 1.6 million people per 25 years. To put this in perspective, note that the 1950 total population of the Extended Washington Area was 1.8 million. It took 150 years to get to 1.8 million, but every 25 years since then we have added nearly the same number of people!

In examining Figure 3-1, an important question to ask is what will the population of the Washington area be in 2050 or 2075? If the trend holds, we will be at 8.3 million by 2050, and by 2075 we will have joined the ranks of the megacities with a population of 10 million people.

Models for a future Washington?
(U.S. megacities; year 1990 metro area populations)

City	Population (million)
Los Angeles	14.5
New York	18.1

U.S. Census Bureau Data (1992 Statistical Abstracts)

National Population Growth

While most industrialized nations of the world are experiencing virtually no population growth or even a population decline, the U.S. is growing rapidly. The U.S. has been adding about 27 million people per decade since 1950, and the Census Bureau projects that we are likely to continue to do so for at least the next hundred years (Figure 3-2). As a result our midyear 2000 population of about 280 million is projected to more than double (to 571 million) by the end of this century.[93]

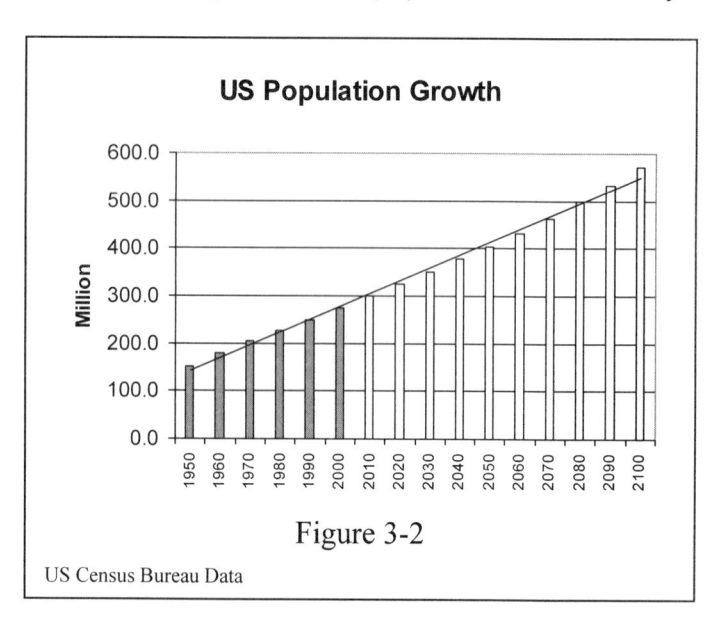

Figure 3-2

US Census Bureau Data

Putting 571 Million in Perspective

The U.S. is a country with a large land area, and because of our extensive land some people appear unconcerned about our population growth. "Our projections for 2100 will give us a population density one-quarter of the United Kingdom," said Frederick W. Hollmann, a Census Bureau demographer. "We'll

Growth Pressures 51

still be a sparsely populated country among the industrialized countries of the world."[94]

While arithmetically correct, this kind of reasoning fails to consider that, unlike the United Kingdom and most other European countries, much of our land area is composed of vast interior arid and semi-arid regions. As a consequence, population densities in the U.S. vary dramatically, with coastal densities far exceeding those of the interior regions. Many of our coastal regions are far from sparsely populated today, and we would be foolish to assume that these desirable regions will not suffer the brunt of a doubling population. Turning our attention to Figure 3-3, we see that Maryland well illustrates the point.

By European Standards Maryland is a Densely Populated Area

□ 1998 ▣ 2025 ■ 2050

People per Square Mile (0–1400)

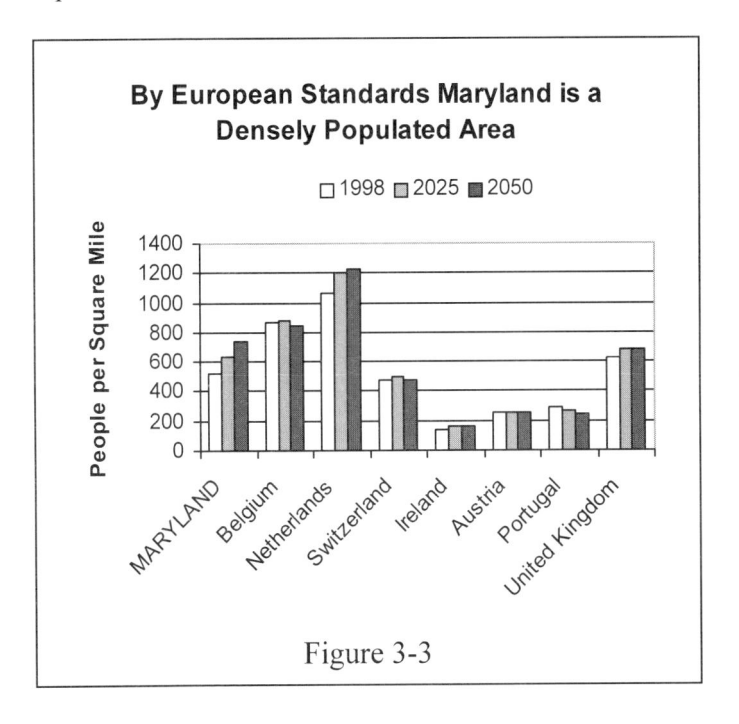

MARYLAND, Belgium, Netherlands, Switzerland, Ireland, Austria, Portugal, United Kingdom

Figure 3-3

Figure 3-3 compares the population density of Maryland to the densities of seven well known European countries.[95] We can see from the figure that the population density of Maryland is already greater than four of these nations. By 2025 it will be nearly equal that of the United Kingdom. And by 2050, Maryland's population density will surpass that of the United Kingdom.[96] In other words, Maryland is already densely populated, and growing more so.

To the people of Maryland and other populous coastal regions, it will not matter that our vast interior regions remain sparsely populated. What matters is the population density of the area that we call home.

While population density is a very relevant measure for people living in crowded coastal regions, it is not the only means of putting a population number in perspective. At the national level a new measure, the ecological footprint, offers a very important insight regarding the size of our population. We will examine this more modern measure in Chapter 4.

Finally, it is interesting to note the historical perspective: our projected year 2100 population is nearly identical to the 1953 population of China.[97] It is hard to imagine that Americans want to follow in the population footsteps of China. Yet, with our current policies and general avoidance of the population growth issue, it could be argued that this is the path we are on.

What's Pushing Us Toward 571 Million?

There are three primary factors pushing us toward doubling our population this century:

1) fertility of the people already in the U.S. and their descendents,
2) net immigration over the 2000 to 2100 period, and
3) fertility of these immigrants and their descendents.

According to Census Bureau projections, each of these three factors will contribute about 1/3 of the projected increase.[98]

Growth Pressures

That is, in "round numbers" each of the three factors will contribute about 100 million people. It probably surprises no one that post-2000 immigrants and their descendents account for most of the projected growth. But it may surprise many to know that even if we were to immediately drive net immigration to zero, we would still add more people to the U.S. over the course of this century than the number of people who reside in Germany today.

It may also surprise many to know that the projected level of immigration does not preclude stabilizing the U.S. population – but more on this topic is reserved for Chapter 6.

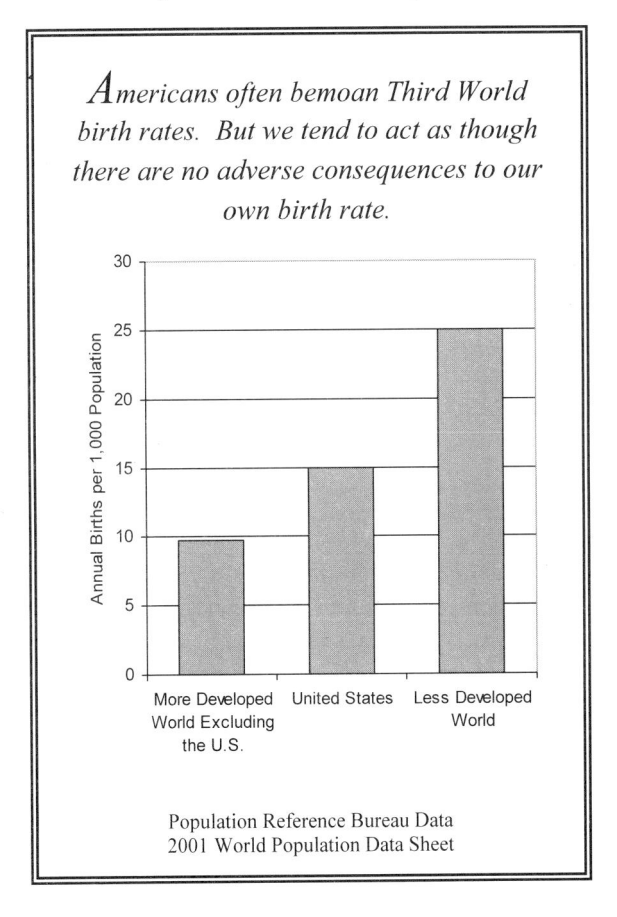

Americans often bemoan Third World birth rates. But we tend to act as though there are no adverse consequences to our own birth rate.

Region	Annual Births per 1,000 Population
More Developed World Excluding the U.S.	~10
United States	~15
Less Developed World	~25

Population Reference Bureau Data
2001 World Population Data Sheet

Choices

It is essential that we recognize that the preceding projections for future populations of the Washington area and the U.S. are not inevitable. Projections for 5 or 10 years into the future may be close to inevitable because our population dynamic is analogous to a very large ship – it takes time to change its course. But projections beyond a decade or two are subject to radical revision.

The Census Bureau takes pains to inform us that there is nothing inevitable about the 571 million population projected for 2100. The number could go much higher if we make the wrong choices. But it could also be much lower. To emphasize the uncertainties involved in making a 100 year projection, the Census Bureau published a Lowest Series and a Highest Series projection – 283 million and 1.2 *billion*, respectively for year 2100.[99] This enormous spread is not a consequence of chance events beyond our control. Rather it stems from the inability to forecast what *choices* our society will make.

Notwithstanding the potential extremes, the middle series projection (571 million in 2100) unquestionably represents the most probable outcome. In part this is so because it is an extension of the path we are already on. In effect it is the path of least resistance. But in the long term, the value of projections is that they provide advance warning about our probable destination. When projections tell us that our current course will place our children in an undesirable environment, we have time to act; we have time to alter course.

"As for the future ... there is a colorful spectrum of possibilities, from the worst to the best. What will happen, I do not know. Hope forces me to believe that those better alternatives will prevail, and above all it forces me to do something to make them happen."

Vaclav Havel
Chapter Nine, *Earth Odyssey*, by Mark Hertsgaard

4
Growth and Economic Wellbeing

"The health of our country does not depend on population growth, nor does the vitality of business, nor the welfare of the average person."

Rockefeller Commission 1972 report
"Population Growth and the American Future"[100]

Local Job Growth and Local Unemployment

As the following excerpt illustrates, anxiety about unemployment dissuades people from critically examining the costs of recruiting new businesses in an already large and prosperous area.

> "Recently, four couples gathered for a pleasant dinner hosted by old friends. ... Later in the evening the conversation turned to roads and the frustrations of driving in the area. When I commented that we were unlikely to lessen our traffic frustrations or constrain sprawl without confronting our rapidly growing regional population, the response was unenthusiastic. Two of the men commented to the effect that it would be better to accept sprawl and congestion than to tamper with growth. Others remained diplomatically silent, and the subject was soon dropped." [101]

Such anxiety might be justified in a small or decaying community. We have all read sad stories of towns that have lost their economic mainstays and become ghost towns, with people having to leave a place they love to support themselves.

But the anxiety seems overwrought in a wealthy, metropolitan area of more than 5 million people. If a healthy community of 5 million does not offer enough employment opportunity, what size will be enough?

Does a high job growth rate offer employment security? While we would naturally expect areas exhibiting greater job growth to exhibit the least unemployment, the evidence shows that among large metropolitan areas, the faster growing areas have no significant advantage. Using 1998 unemployment data for the 26 metropolitan areas with a workforce greater than 1 million, we see from Figure 4-1 that the average unemployment rate varies little between the 13 faster growing areas and 13 slower growing areas – even though the difference in rate of job growth is very substantial.[102] Thus, recent data show that intense employment growth has had little impact on the unemployment rates.

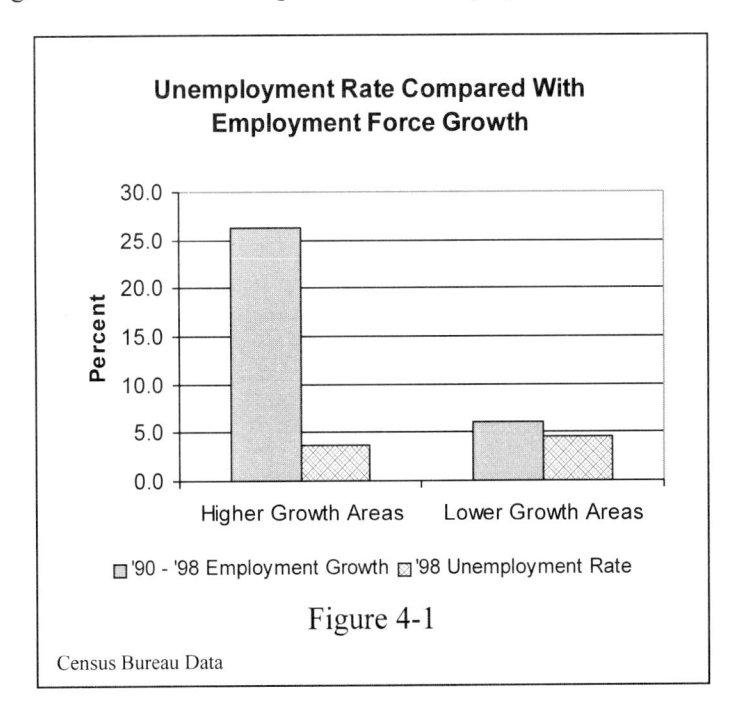

Unemployment Rate Compared With Employment Force Growth

Figure 4-1

Census Bureau Data

An important point to take from Figure 4-1 is the enormous job growth of the 13 higher growth areas – averaging more than 25% in just 8 years. With such a large increase in so short a time there can be no doubt of the toll taken on these communities, in terms of congestion, infrastructure lagging the exploding population, and loss of natural amenities. An explosion of new residents rushing in to fill new jobs means extraordinary demands for new schools, wider roads, extra police and other government expenses that come with population growth. Yet for all of the costs of fast growth, the improvement in unemployment is marginal.

We all want jobs, and many of us prefer not to relocate to a different area when we find ourselves searching for a job. Hence few of us question spokespersons for the Growth Machine when they tout efforts to recruit corporations and jobs into an area. But in spite of our hopes, relatively few local residents see any lasting benefit. According to Timothy Bartik, economist with the Upjohn Institute for Employment Research, and an authority on development: "In the long run, if you create five jobs, four of them go to people who otherwise would be living someplace else."[103] Even in the short term, nearly half of these new jobs are filled by people who move in to fill them.[104] Thus the more jobs we lure to our metropolitan area, the more people will move in to fill them. The net result is that unemployment rates remain essentially unaffected – while our congestion and related quality of living losses are permanently ratcheted up a notch.

Population Growth and Economic Growth

We are a growth-oriented culture. It has been said that while our official motto is "In God We Trust," our operative motto is "In Growth We Trust."[105] Our historic aim has been a better standard of living for all Americans, i.e., per capita economic growth. But the term "growth" has such a powerful positive connotation that popular thinking is often uncritical. Population Growth does tend to increase *total* economic growth, but as we shall soon see it does not necessarily improve *per capita* economic growth. Unfortunately, relatively few people make this distinction, and consequently many Americans fear that their economic wellbeing would be sacrificed if population growth were curtailed. With such a mindset these people are reluctant to confront the downsides of rapid population growth or support any steps to stabilize U.S. population.

As noted in the subchapter that follows (An Ethical Threshold) there are questions about how much more total economic growth we can ethically sustain. But for present purposes let us assume such questions are moot, and consider only the question: Do we need population growth in order to have per capita economic growth?

To answer this question we will first compare major metropolitan areas in the U.S., and then we will consider the U.S. in relation to western European countries.

Metropolitan Area Growth. Local politicians and chambers of commerce often proclaim that our only choices are growth or atrophy. Such pronouncements echo the conventional wisdom (and promote the Growth Machine agenda), but the evidence seems to be lacking. In a recent Brookings Institution study, "Growth Without Growth," the growth statistics of the hundred largest metropolitan areas in the U.S. were examined. The purpose was to determine if there is any evidence supporting the notion that population growth is necessary for increased personal economic wellbeing.

The measure of personal economic wellbeing selected was per capita income. To see if population growth is a good predictor of per capita economic growth, the data for each city was plotted in a scatter diagram (Figure 4-2). Each dot in the diagram represents a single city. The position of the dot along the horizontal axis represents the population growth rate; the position along the vertical axis represents the per capita income growth rate. If there were good correlation between the two types of growth, the dots would cluster tightly around the trendline, and the R^2 value would be much closer to 1 than 0.

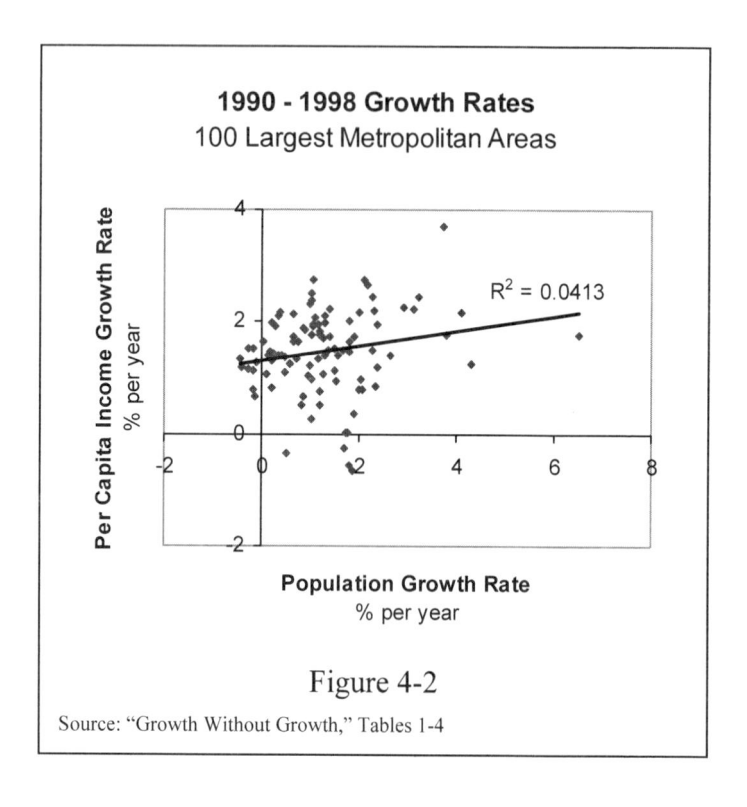

Figure 4-2

Source: "Growth Without Growth," Tables 1-4

Growth and Economic Wellbeing 61

We see clearly from Figure 4-2 that there is negligible correlation between population growth and per capita income growth, i.e., population growth is a poor predictor of per capita income growth.[106] In the words of the study author: "We have punctured one important piece of conventional wisdom: the idea that achieving income growth in a metropolitan area requires population growth."

"Growth Without Growth" goes on to note that 23 of the metropolitan areas had personal economic growth above the median *and* population growth below the median. For policy makers faced with citizen complaints about loss of open space, road congestion, and school overcrowding, these 23 areas represent the ideal to be sought: economic growth with little or no population growth. The policies to produce this ideal are still being researched, but it is clear that the study gives policy makers ample reason to eschew the conventional wisdom and seek more effective strategies.

National Growth. To examine the question at the national level, population growth and economic growth were examined for the United States and the fifteen western European countries noted below.

Austria	Germany	Portugal
Belgium	Greece	Spain
Denmark	Italy	Sweden
Finland	Netherlands	Switzerland
France	Norway	United Kingdom

The period of growth considered is essentially 1970 – 2000. The measure of economic growth used is per capita Gross Domestic Product as provided by the U.S. Census Bureau.[107] The result is shown in Figure 4-3. Each point in the figure represents one of the 16 countries. The rightmost point corresponds to the U.S. – highest population growth by far, but average per capita economic growth.

Note that the trendline is nearly horizontal and the R^2 value is nearly zero; these attributes signify that there is no significant correlation between per capita economic growth and population growth. That is, the data strongly contradict any notion that higher population growth rates are important contributors to greater per capita economic prosperity.

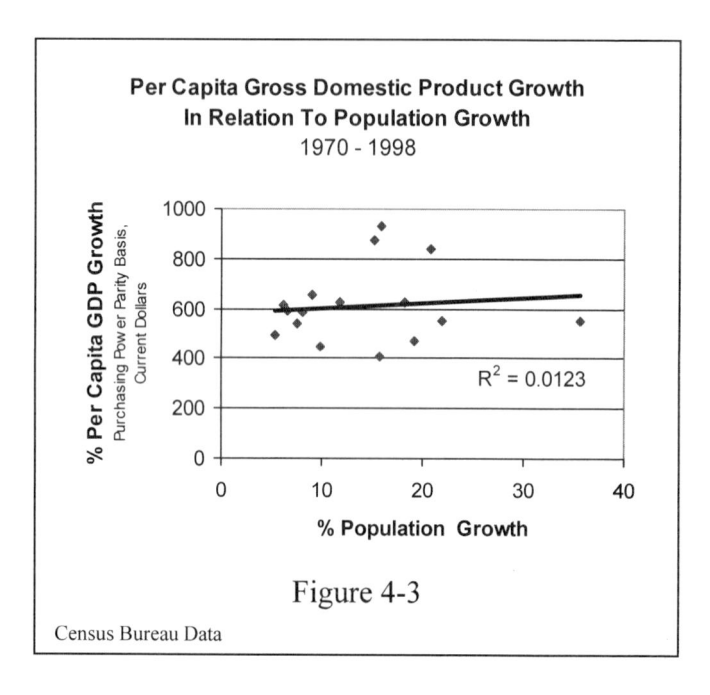

**Per Capita Gross Domestic Product Growth
In Relation To Population Growth
1970 - 1998**

$R^2 = 0.0123$

% Population Growth

Figure 4-3

Census Bureau Data

The negligible correlation between population growth and per capita economic growth at both the national and the major metropolitan area levels should give anyone ample reason to reconsider blind belief in the notion that population growth is necessary for economic wellbeing. This lack of correlation should help all of us heed the words of the Rockefeller Commission: neither the health of our country nor the welfare of the average person depends on population growth.

A Red Herring

Our aging population and its impact on Social Security are sometimes cited as reasons that we must grow our population. Such a prescription serves mainly to divert our attention from the fact that a day of reckoning is unavoidable.

The only question is will we face that day or will we shift it to our descendents?

See Appendix C.

An Ethical Threshold

When asked whether President George W. Bush would call on drivers to reduce their fuel consumption, White House press secretary Ari Fleischer responded: "That's a big no. The president believes that it's an American way of life, and that it should be the goal of policymakers to protect the American way of life. The American way of life is a blessed one."[108]

Mr. Fleischer's statement surely deserves a place in the annals of shallow optimism. Not only does it ignore the environmental consequences of our way of life, but it also ignores the adverse consequences for other peoples of the world.

In large measure, our 'blessed' way of life is defined by extraordinary per capita consumption of both non-renewable and renewable resources. The environmental consequences of our consumption are often decried. And given that 1.1 billion of the world's 6 billion people live with hunger and fear of starvation,[109] our compassion for others is often questioned.

Doubt about our compassion for people in other lands may soon deepen. We are about to cross a threshold that dramatically raises the ethical stakes. It is one thing to live lavishly from our own renewable resources while other people are in need. It is another thing entirely when satisfaction of our way of life causes us to usurp the resources of other lands needed by other people.

Barring a change in current trends, increased U.S. consumption will result in increased poverty for other peoples of the world. The basis for this assertion is the estimated biological productive capacities and the 'ecological footprints' of the U.S. and the other nations of the world.

Growth and Economic Wellbeing 65

The ecological footprint (EF) is a measure of the per capita consumption of a population. EF is defined as the per capita area of land (and sea) required to support the consumptive habits of a population. It is measured in hectares per person (1 hectare = 2.5 acres), and has six components: cropland area, grazing land area, forest area, fishing area, built-up land, and land area necessary for sequestering CO_2.

The EF for virtually all countries has been estimated from United Nations statistics. Similarly, the biological productive capacities of these countries have also been estimated. Few regions of the world have an ecological footprint that fits within their biological capacity. The primary reason for the capacity deficit is inadequate biomass to sequester the CO_2 from fossil fuel consumption.

But when CO_2 sequestration is removed from consideration, the opposite is true. At the moment, most regions of the world have an ecological footprint (excluding CO_2 sequestration) that does fit within their biological capacity. Unfortunately this is about to change, particularly in the United States.

In 1996 the U.S. had a modest surplus of biological capacity (excluding CO_2 sequestration), but this surplus is rapidly transforming into a huge deficit. Without dramatic changes in our per capita consumption, population growth, and/or the available biological technology, *by 2100 our aggregate consumption will be nearly twice our productive capacity* (Figure 4-4).[110]

We in the U.S., and other wealthy nations, are able to live beyond our biological means by importing what we need. This is simply a matter of trade when worldwide per capita biological resources are plentiful. But with the world population jumping from 6 to 9 billion over the next 50 years, and all the developing nations seeking desperately to push per capita consumption above the poverty level, biological resources are anything but plentiful.

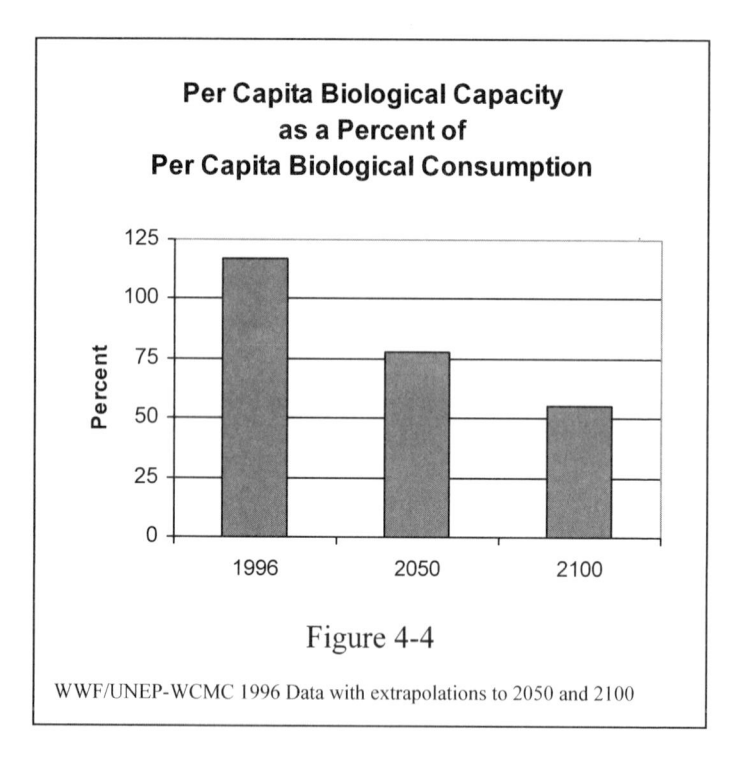

Per Capita Biological Capacity as a Percent of Per Capita Biological Consumption

Figure 4-4

WWF/UNEP-WCMC 1996 Data with extrapolations to 2050 and 2100

Even basic food resources may not be adequate to support a world population of 9 or 10 billion. The world's per capita area of land in grain production has been declining steadily in recent years, ... chiefly because the world population continues to grow while almost all arable land is already under cultivation. The late Henry W. Kendall, Nobel Prize-winning physicist at the Massachusetts Institute of Technology and chairman of the Union of Concerned Scientists, and David Pimentel, professor of ecology and agricultural science at Cornell University, found that "the human race now appears to be getting close to the limits of global food productive capacity based on present technologies." Although a doubling of food production by 2050 is achievable in principle, "the elements to accomplish it are not now in place or on the way ..."[111]

Growth and Economic Wellbeing

Thus, continued high consumption in conjunction with continued rapid population growth in the U.S. will limit the resources available to people in less fortunate nations. We will simply price people of developing nations out of the market.

When we think about pricing poorer people out of the market for goods they need worse than we, we are confronted with an ethical question. How can we ethically grow our population without reducing our consumption by a proportionate amount? Ethically, we must halve our consumption if we are going to double our population. Or if we are unwilling to halve our consumption, then we must stop our population from doubling.

Of course we can assume that our biological productivity will double somehow, and the ethical threshold thereby avoided. In this way, dealing with the issue could be somewhat comfortably avoided. But making such an assumption is clearly a gamble. And if we are honest, we know that if the gamble is lost, it is our grandchildren and their children who will pay for our evasion. Our legacy to them will be an unavoidable choice: drastically cut consumption, or acknowledge their moral standing as usurpers of the resources that the world's poor desperately need.

"A world where some live in comfort and plenty, while half of the human race lives on less than $2 a day is neither just, nor stable."

President Bush speaking before the World Bank in July, as quoted in the *Christian Science Monitor*, "Time to get serious on global hunger," Michael Taylor, October 29, 2001

5

Growth Politics

> *"All politics is local."*
> Tip O'Neil, Speaker of the U.S. House of Representatives, 1977 – 1986

The Greater Washington Board of Trade (BOT) is heavily involved in promoting highway projects in the Washington area. A highway of particular interest to the BOT is the so-called 'Techway,' a highway and bridge proposal to link the Dulles area of Virginia with the Gaithersburg area of Maryland. In promoting the Techway, the BOT (and/or its leading members) have used radio program appearances, the web site endgridlock.org, press conferences, and letters published in local newspapers.

In May 2001, Congressman Frank Wolf asked the Federal Highway Administration to cancel its study of the Techway – a study that Congressman Wolf had initiated. His reversal was precipitated by an outcry from homeowners who would be adversely affected by the Techway. In explaining his change of mind, he stated that "I was astounded by the number of potential crossing alignments. The neighborhoods and federal and local parklands and wetlands that would have been affected were extensive. ... I make my decisions based on what I think is right. In this case, I do not think it is right to hurt area residents who have put a lot of money and effort into their homes..."[112]

In response to this political setback, the BOT dramatically stepped up its effort with a May 30, 2001 e-mail from John Kane (then Chairman, BOT Transportation and Environment Committee) to all members of the Board of Trade. The e-mail began by referencing Congressman Wolf's reversal and the need to instill a political will for the Techway. The main purpose of the e-mail was to urge executives to recruit their employees to the Endgridlock.org organization. The conclusion of the e-mail included the following:[113]

> "You can make a difference by taking the following steps.
>
> 1) At the bottom of this e-mail, you will find a draft message that you should send to your employees showing your interest in Endgridlock.org and urging them to join. ...
>
> 2) Next, please send this e-mail to your employees through your own e-mail system. To highlight participation and show your personal commitment, *you might even suggest that employees who join Endgridlock.org will be entered into a pool with the lucky winner getting a day off.*" (emphasis added)

The BOT membership includes 1,300 corporations employing hundreds of thousands of people. Mr. Kane's e-mail was clearly intended to use the lobbying strength, the numerical and financial superiority, of the BOT without regard for the thousands of people who had expressed outrage over the threat of lost property values and diminished quality of living. His e-mail is a revealing example of the "Growth Machine" at work.

In 1976 Harvey Molotch wrote a ground breaking essay titled: "The City as Growth Machine." In it he bluntly asserted that:

> A city is conceived as the expression of the interests of some land-based elite who profit through the increasing intensification of the land use of the area in which its members hold a common interest. An elite competes with other land-based elites in an effort to have *growth-inducing resources* invested within its own area as opposed to that of another.

Moreover governmental authority, at the local and non-local levels, is utilized to assist in achieving this growth at the expense of competing localities.[114]

In a 1993 book, Altshuler and Gomez-Ibanez followed suit with an equally blunt assertion:

> Throughout American history the most consistent theme in local governance has been the pursuit of growth: more people, more jobs, and more real estate development. Local democracy has been dominated by "growth coalitions," composed of individuals and enterprises with a direct stake in real estate development.[115]

Readers who have witnessed explosive sprawl and deplored the concomitant loss of quality of living in the Washington area may readily resonate with these views. On the other hand the growth coalitions have done such a masterful job of promoting growth, that few people recognize who benefits and who pays.

Historically, Americans have tended to accept growth promotions without critical appraisal. In part this is because of "tenets deeply rooted in American culture: a craving for boundless growth, a perception of unlimited land and economic resources."[116] It is also due to anxiety about employment security and the possibility of having to relocate in order to stay employed. According to Molotch, "it is probably this very anxiety which often leads workers, or at least their union spokespeople, to support enthusiastically employers' preferred policies of growth."

"The engine of the growth machine is powered by the fortunes resulting from land speculation and real estate development."[117] The primary beneficiaries are the speculators, developers, mortgage bankers, realtors, and the local construction and construction supply firms. The local business community at large also supports the Growth Machine since the conventional wisdom is that growth will increase business volume, and hence the wealth of the business owners. (In reality, these dreams of greater wealth often fall victim to larger competitors attracted by the growth.)

The major growth machine players tend to be wealthy, well organized, and politically influential in their communities. They advance their interests through organizations such as the Board of Trade, Chambers of Commerce, Association of Realtors, and the Home Builders Association. The pro-growth mission of these organizations is often quite public. A sampling of statements from Washington area Growth Machine organizations, including local governments, is provided in Appendix A.

The target of growth coalition efforts is typically local government. Pro-growth business interests recognize the important role that local government has in the business of land development (e.g., zoning and building permits) and paying for the infrastructure (e.g., roads) that is a pre-condition for growth. Hence, these organizations attempt to use local governments to gain the resources and regulations that will enhance the growth potential.

The local governments are almost always willing supporters of the pro-growth elite because growth means more tax revenue. Indeed, the Planning Commissioner's Journal identifies pursuit of greater tax revenues as one of the root causes of sprawl.[118]

In the Washington area and similarly wealthy areas around the country, the target of the pro-growth promotional efforts is increasingly the general public. As noted in the Sprawl subchapter (trend toward growth control measures at the ballot box), the public is becoming resistive to growth. People are beginning to see that while growth typically benefits only a small proportion of local residents, it almost always brings with it the problems of increased air and water pollution, traffic congestion, and destruction of natural amenities.

These quality of living costs become increasingly important among a prosperous, mobile population. Hence, resistance to pro-growth measures desired by the business elite is growing. This resistance is usually in the form of pressure on the local government, and can lead to expulsion of elected officials sympathetic to the pro-growth side.[119] Consequently, the pro-growth forces are finding it necessary to go beyond influencing local government. They must also mount campaigns to influence the general public. One member of the Greater Washington Board of Trade spent $140,000 of his own money for radio advertising to counter resistance to new roads.[120]

The Game of Economic Development

The growth machine function of local governments is carried out most conspicuously by the Economic Development agencies. Advertisements placed by economic development agencies of a local or state government are readily found in magazines and other media. These ads are run even if the locality is already growing rapidly or full to over flowing with people and businesses. The Pacific Northwest population is growing much faster than the nation as a whole, yet local economic development agencies are still running ads touting the area as a great place to live and work.[121] The County of Fairfax, Va. is both highly prosperous and "full to the brim" with people and businesses, yet the County's Economic Development Authority is spending millions of dollars to advertise. In 2000, Fairfax County's $1.6 million "E-Country" ad campaign was the ninth in a series over 22 years promoting Fairfax as the place to do business.[122]

Economic development as practiced by local and state governments most often takes the form of offering corporations and businesses incentives to locate in or expand in a particular area. The incentives are generally financial in nature and amount to millions of taxpayer dollars per year in our area alone.

Certainly there is often a strong case for incentives to locate in depressed inner city areas or in cities that are suffering a serious loss of their traditional economic base. But when applied to major metropolitan areas with an existing, robust economy, the incentives generally benefit only a few at the expense of the larger community.

In 1999, the *Baltimore Sun's* Jay Hancock wrote a fine series of articles exposing the flaws in the practice of economic development. His articles demonstrate what Molotch said 23 years earlier: local growth does not make jobs: it distributes jobs. His articles vividly illustrate that flawed economic development programs waste tax dollars, subsidize layoffs of thousands of people in other areas, and increase the demand for expensive public services in the area "developed."

An example case used in the series involved Rite Aid Corp. When the drugstore executives flew into Harford, MD, to look at prospective sites for a new warehouse, they were looking for more than location. They were also looking for Maryland taxpayers to write a big check to help pay for the warehouse.

By pitting Maryland against Virginia, Rite Aid obtained millions of dollars in grants and tax breaks. Maryland won the warehouse and 850 jobs – but Rite Aid's secret, two-stage auction prompted the state to pay almost double what Virginia was offering.

> "On March 21, 1997, [Governor] Glendening announced 'wonderful news for Maryland.' Rite Aid was bringing 850 'family-supporting jobs' to the state, he said. It was 'one of the most significant job-creation announcements in the last five years.'
>
> He didn't mention how expensive Maryland's Rite Aid bid was compared with Virginia's, or how Rite Aid probably would have come to Maryland without

incentives. ... He didn't point out that the news was not wonderful for hundreds of workers in Harrisburg, Pa., where Rite Aid shut down an older facility..., and in Putnam County, W.Va. where a warehouse will be closed..." [123]

In addition to dealing with the job creation myth, Hancock's series deals clearly with the fact that recruiting businesses increases the population and services demand of an area:

> "New businesses cause population growth even if the workers they hire already live in the region. ... 'If somebody moves from the local McDonald's to take a job at the plant, and somebody else moves from out of state to work at McDonald's, that plant has generated a new state resident.' ...
>
> Public officials often praise marked-down taxes from new businesses as 'money we wouldn't have had otherwise.' ... But what communities should ask themselves, critics say, is not whether the money is new, but whether it will cover the costs [of services to new residents] that will come with it.'"[124]

The questionable economics of luring businesses with subsidies is not unknown in state and local governments. Even some elected officials who energetically recruit corporations have their doubts about the practice. For example, in stark contrast to the tone and text of his Rite-Aid speech, Governor Glendening supports federal legislation that would curtail corporate give-away programs.[125]

Even if the new tax revenue covers the costs of the services provided to the new business and new residents, a positive economic case would not necessarily mean that recruiting the new business is in the best interest of the community. Communities should also ask themselves if continuous recruiting of new businesses and the resultant population increase adds to or detracts from their overall quality of life.

From Community Benefit to Pyramid Scheme

Many of us have family or friends who live in an economically marginal community. Often the community is small and has fallen on hard times because a key local industry has collapsed. In communities of this sort, the efforts of the local Growth Machine can only be applauded as efforts that will benefit the entire community.

But in large urban areas with a diverse business base, the efforts of the Growth Machine often slip from civic benefit to self-serving. Those of us who live in a large and economically robust area such as Washington may want to keep the words of Oregonian activist Andy Kerr in mind when listening to pro-growth promotions. "Urban growth is a pyramid scheme in which a relative few make a killing, some others make a living, but most [of us] pay for it."[126]

> "*There* are no reasonably accurate estimates of the amount of money states shovel out [for economic development]. That's because few want to know. ... All that's certain is the figure is many billions of dollars each year."
>
> Time Magazine, "Corporate Welfare,"
> by Donald L. Bartlett and James B. Steele,
> November 1998.

6

Toward a Better Future

Restraining the Growth Machine

The Growth Machine is a leading reason that major urban areas experience population growth, sprawl, and congestion. This subchapter briefly sketches three approaches to restraining the Growth Machine so that the interests of the full community are served. This subchapter also introduces the "fair share" growth threshold, and it concludes with comments regarding the relative merits of regional and jurisdictional approaches to restraining the machine.

The three approaches are not anti-business. Even the Washington area would suffer if it were perceived as anti-business. As businesses fail with changing times or competitive pressures, the community must be seen as an attractive place for other businesses to locate. When choosing a location, businesses evaluate many factors – including subsidies that a community may offer. But according to fiscal analyst Don Carrington, incentives usually do not sway a location decision.[127] And in an area such as Washington, it would be absurd to claim that taxpayer subsidies are necessary in order for the area to be attractive to businesses. Restraining the Growth Machine's access to taxpayer dollars is not anti-business; it is a step toward a better community for all of us.

Approach 1 – Restrain new businesses recruitment

While the link between business recruitment and sprawl is seldom discussed, it is no secret either. A member of the Virginia House recently said counties should not complain about development on the one hand and try to lure new companies on the other. "I sit up here in amazement. I will believe a county is serious about trying to control [population] growth when they stop trying to attract it."[128]

It is difficult to reconcile the practice of spending tax dollars to attract new businesses at the same time we are spending tax dollars to mitigate the congestion and loss of open space caused by the addition of new businesses to the area. Yet, economic-development agencies are an integral part of all our local governments, and their budgets are in the millions of dollars per year. "Every jurisdiction ... is out trying to attract new companies and ready to pop the cork when it scores."[129]

While the activities of these agencies include re-development of economically distressed areas, their prime mission is attracting new companies, and consequently more residents, solely for the sake of aggregate economic growth.

In counties suffering from congestion and other ills of excessive growth, business recruitment not specifically targeted for economically distressed areas has outlived its usefulness. Yet it continues. The alleged reason is economic benefits to the counties. But these "benefits" are estimated without any accounting in regard to lost open space, congestion, overcrowding of schools, etc. Even the claimed economic benefits are highly questionable. The literature on the subject shows the difficulty in making a convincing case. According to researcher Roland Stephen, "economic theory and many empirical studies indicate that the aggregate economic gains from such [economic development] policies are very uncertain."[130] Mr. Stephen asks: Why do politicians adopt costly policies that yield uncertain economic benefits? His answer: politics.

In the second half of 2000, Montgomery County Executive, Douglas Duncan, proposed to provide cash to unprofitable high-tech startups in order to boost Maryland's profile as a haven for technology. According to Duncan, everywhere he travels in the state, people are asking, "How can we get these technology companies here?"

If we needed business growth, Mr. Duncan's focus on technology might have merit. Technology companies are attractive in comparison to other businesses because they generally bring higher paying jobs. Therefore the ratio of tax revenue to services cost for each new employee is favorable compared to warehousing, manufacturing, or the like. But in an already prosperous and congested area, this advantage does not mean that luring new technology businesses with taxpayer dollars will benefit the larger community.

Steven Walters, an economics professor at Loyola College of Maryland said, "This [Duncan's proposal] is corporate welfare, pure and simple." David Brunori, an adjunct professor teaching state and local tax law at George Washington University Law School in Washington, D.C., said, "This is just another attempt at throwing money at companies when there is no need to."[131]

Mr. Duncan's proposal is not unusual. It is a routine example of business recruitment guided by the aims of the Growth Machine. To end the dominance of the Growth Machine we need to start asking our county and state representatives: Why should we use tax dollars to recruit new businesses when the result will be more congestion and less open space? If the answer offered is 'more tax revenue is required to sustain our quality of life,' we need to note that since 1950 the Washington area population jumped from under 2 million to over 5 million, and ask: If growth is the solution, why do we still have fiscal concerns after 50 years of mushrooming growth?

Approach 2 – Make new development pay its way

Several years ago Professor Albert Bartlett was discussing the population growth of Boulder with a prominent member of the Colorado Legislature. At one point the legislator said: "Al, we could not stop Boulder's growth if we wanted to!"

Toward a Better Future

Professor Bartlett responded: "I agree, therefore let's put a tax on the growth so that, as a minimum, the growth pays for itself, instead of having to be paid for by the existing taxpayers."

The legislator's response was quick and emphatic: "*You can't do that; you'd slow down our growth!*"[132]

A growing population demands an expanding infrastructure and results in a continuous burden of capital costs. Infrastructure examples include:

Schools	Sanitary Sewer Systems
Fire Protection Facilities	Water Treatment Facilities
Police Facilities and Jails	Recreation Facilities
Utility Distribution Systems	Libraries
Roads and Other Transportation Facilities	Solid Waste Disposal Systems

According to Maryland's Governor Glendening, each new classroom costs $90,000; every mile of new sewer line costs $200,000, and every lane-mile of highway costs $4 million. In Virginia, fast growing Loudoun County is planning to spend $660 million to build 26 schools over the next six years, and Loudoun's property tax rate has already risen 30% in the past decade.[133]

The near universal norm in the U.S. is that the costs of infrastructure to support new development are shared among all taxpayers. How much is the annual cost of growth to existing residents of the Washington area? No one knows. This lack of knowledge also seems to be the norm. Such information is seldom sought by local governments. But it is possible to obtain.

In February 2002, Fodor & Associates of Eugene, Oregon released a major report on growth subsidies in Oregon. The report concluded that the year 2000 growth subsidies in the state of Oregon totaled $1.03 billion. This equates to a subsidy of about $18,000 per new arrival.[134]

If these costs were levied predominantly on newly developed business facilities, the price of these facilities would go up; the market for new development would be cooled, and regional population growth would be slowed – just as the Colorado legislator speaking with Professor Bartlett feared.[135]

In Montgomery County, MD, subsidized growth is routine, but there is at least a focus on orderly development. The county has had an adequate public facilities (APF) law since 1973. The intent of the law is to restrict new development to those areas with the necessary infrastructure. The County publishes an annual "Growth Policy Report" which defines the capacity of public facilities in various areas of the county to accommodate new development. The report provides developers with advance notice of those areas of the county in which development projects are likely to receive approval.

The capacity ratings are tied to the Capital Improvement Program so that the ratings change annually to reflect new investment in public facilities. However, as funding for public improvements has become progressively more elusive, the APF regulations have induced a few developers eager to start their projects to shoulder more of the infrastructure burden created by proposed projects.[136]

With its APF planning tools it would be a technically modest step for Montgomery County to go from managed growth to growth that is not subsidized by the resident taxpayers. What is lacking is an adequately informed citizenry that will demand an end to the subsidies that promote growth, sprawl, and congestion.

In other jurisdictions the possibility of making development pay its way may be more remote. In Virginia, effective adequate public facilities requirements are generally not available to the counties. Counties wishing to manage their growth must petition the General Assembly for authority to enact APF ordinances that go beyond rezoning applications.[137] But with Northern Virginia sprawl and congestion spiraling out of control, Northern Virginians may break the grip of Richmond politicians.

Approach 3 – Elect public officials whose campaign funding is not dominated by Growth Machine money

People in local politics often come from a business, real estate, or development background. Their personal wealth is linked to the Growth Machine, and some view the world through this lens. For these politicians, population growth is the engine of prosperity, and they rank growth significantly above citizen concerns about congestion and lost open space.

Politicians, particularly incumbents, typically receive a substantial portion of their campaign financing from members of the Growth Machine. By way of illustration, consider the following examples.

> Among the many campaign contributions Montgomery County Councilman Howard Denis received from the development community in 2000, one was from a well known *out of state* (Virginia) developer[138] who had publicly ridiculed Montgomery County's efforts to preserve open space in the upper county.[139]

> According to *The Washington Post*, Montgomery County Executive Duncan's fundraising in the last year shows that he has "relied heavily on people, companies and political action committees that directly benefit from his pro-growth agenda."[140]

These two examples are not unusual, and there is no intent to suggest that constituents vote for whoever may challenge these two well known officials in the next election. They were selected simply to illustrate the near universal connection between local politicians and the land owners, developers, real estate firms, construction companies, etc. who profit from growth. But if we are to end the practice of using our taxes to import more congestion, crowded schools, and lost open space, the general citizenry must become an effective counterbalance to the wealthy people who profit from growth.

The only way to do this is through the election process. We must press for campaign finance reform. We must tell the candidates that we want an end to using tax dollars to import congestion, lost open space, etc. And whenever we have a well qualified candidate who is not bound by philosophy or money to the Growth Machine, we must get the vote out for that candidate.

Fair Share

Americans must live someplace. So if an urban area's population is growing at a rate no greater than the national population growth rate, it may be said that the area is simply accepting its fair share (or less) of the expanding U.S. population. For areas of this sort, working to control the Growth Machine could be viewed as unnecessary or even misguided. On the other hand, if an area is accepting significantly more than its share of the expanding national population, there is no doubt about the appropriateness of working to restrain the Growth Machine.

From 1975 to 2000 the population of the Extended Washington Area climbed from 3.56 to 5.13 million people. Had the Washington area population increased at the same rate as the national population, our 2000 population would have been 4.52 million people (Figure 6-1). In the last 25 years alone, the Washington area has accepted more than 0.6 million people above its share of the expanding national population.

Toward a Better Future

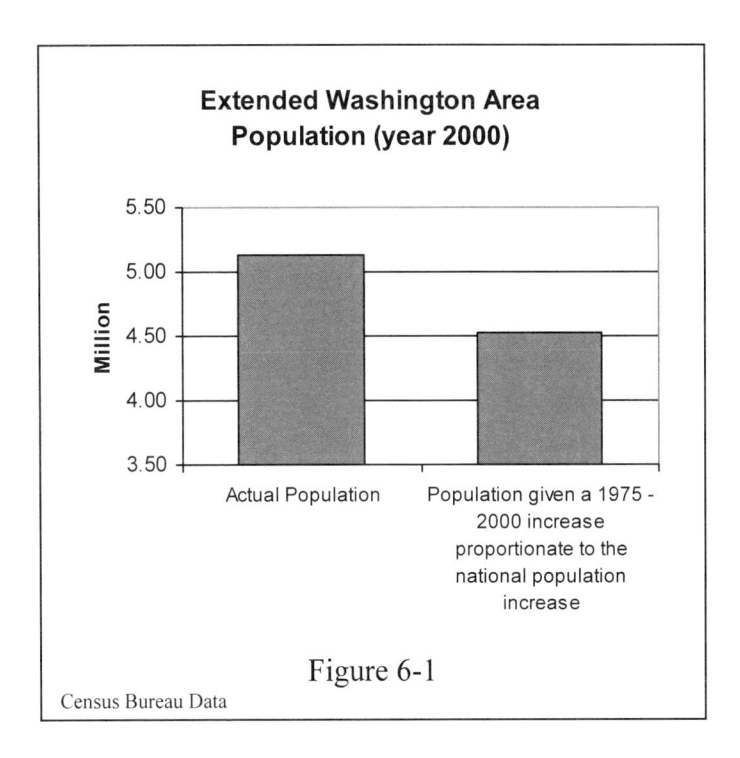

Extended Washington Area Population (year 2000)

[Bar chart showing Actual Population at approximately 5.1 million and Population given a 1975-2000 increase proportionate to the national population increase at approximately 4.5 million]

Figure 6-1

Census Bureau Data

If 0.6 million does not sound like a lot to you, think of this: If we turned all of I495 (beltway) and all of I270 (from the beltway to Frederick) into a giant parking lot, we could not accommodate even half of the cars belonging to the 0.6 million people.

Of course, the 0.6 million beyond "fair share" is not due entirely to the Growth Machine. Other factors include:

- Business advantages of proximity to the federal government
- Natural and cultural amenities of the area.

No data is available to apportion the additional 0.6 million people among the three factors. And to a large extent the apportionment is irrelevant. In any area experiencing growth well above "fair share" it makes sense to end the subsidies that promote growth. If the subsidies are responsible for a significant amount of the growth, then we will achieve a beneficial reduction in the growth rate. If the growth rate is independent of the subsidies, we will at least save tax dollars for a more useful purpose.

Divide and Conquer

If the three approaches just described were implemented successfully in one jurisdiction, say Montgomery County, but not in surrounding jurisdictions, Montgomery County would have only limited cause for celebration. The reason is that induced job and population growth would continue in nearby jurisdictions. Everyone in the Washington region lives in the same Chesapeake Bay watershed, the same atmospheric system, and the same transportation network. Consequently, the Washington *regional* quality of living would continue to decline, and Montgomery County itself would continue to suffer as well (e.g., increased traffic, increased air pollution, increased drought concerns, etc.).

Since little benefit will accrue until the Growth Machine is reined in all over the Washington area, a regional authority could be helpful. Unfortunately such help is unlikely. While there is precedent for regional authorities (for example Metro in Portland, Oregon and SANDAG in San Diego, CA) there appears to be no precedent for a regional authority that is doing more than trying to accommodate more and more businesses and people through "Smart Growth." Why is this? One reason is the Growth Machine. Smart Growth may be an irritant to part of the machine, but as practiced to date, Smart Growth is essentially compatible with the machine's primary objective of more businesses and more people. On the other hand, slowing growth by ending subsidies is inimical to this objective, and no Growth Machine would stand idly by while a regional authority is chartered to do so.

Attempting to restrain the Growth Machine via a regional authority is therefore a dubious strategy. Following a variation of the old maxim of "divide and conquer" is probably the only reasonable course. The area is already divided into distinct jurisdictions, and for opposing the Growth Machine we should endeavor to keep it that way. Once a county is subsumed into a regional authority, the power of the county voter will be immediately diminished (diluted), and the ability of the Growth Machine to concentrate its resources will be immediately enhanced. The members of the Growth Machine know this, and this is at least part of the reason that machine stalwarts such as John Kane and Montgomery County Executive Duncan advocate a regional transportation authority.[141]

When we focus narrowly on managing growth, there is a risk that we unconsciously become blind to some of the root causes of sprawl.

In the booklet "Getting to Smart Growth," 100 policies for implementing Smart Growth are itemized. Not one of these policies advocates ending the growth subsidies that contribute to the problems Smart Growth is trying to mitigate.

The booklet was published January 2002, by the Smart Growth Network

Confronting Our National Population Growth

It is clear that if our national population continues to grow at a rapid pace, few metropolitan areas will be able to escape a flood of new residents, and therefore the hard fought efforts to preserve open space and stop the worsening congestion will ultimately fall far short of expectations. If we are to fulfill the promise of Smart Growth, it is imperative that we stabilize our national population.

The Census Bureau projection of 571 million people by 2100 is not inevitable. Our growing population is a matter of choice. We choose our population growth through programs (or lack of programs) that influence fertility levels, immigration policies, or a combination of these means.

Though it may surprise many, stabilizing our national population does not require reducing net immigration below the current level. Our current net immigration is just under 1 million per year and our current total fertility rate is about 2.05 children per woman.[142] If we were to establish and maintain a fertility rate of just under 1.8 children per woman, we would soon stabilize our population – even with a net immigration of 1 million per year. This surprising fact is illustrated in Figure 6-2.

Both curves of Figure 6-2 project U.S. population growth assuming a constant net immigration of 1 million per year.[143] In fact, the demographic input data used to generate the two curves is identical except for the fertility assumptions. *(See Appendix B for a listing of the demographic assumptions used to generate Figure 6-2, and a brief explanation of how fertility rates and immigration levels interact.)*

The key to the dramatic difference in the two curves is that Census Bureau Working Paper (WP) 38 projects that U.S.

fertility will climb quickly from 2.05 to more than 2.2 children per woman.

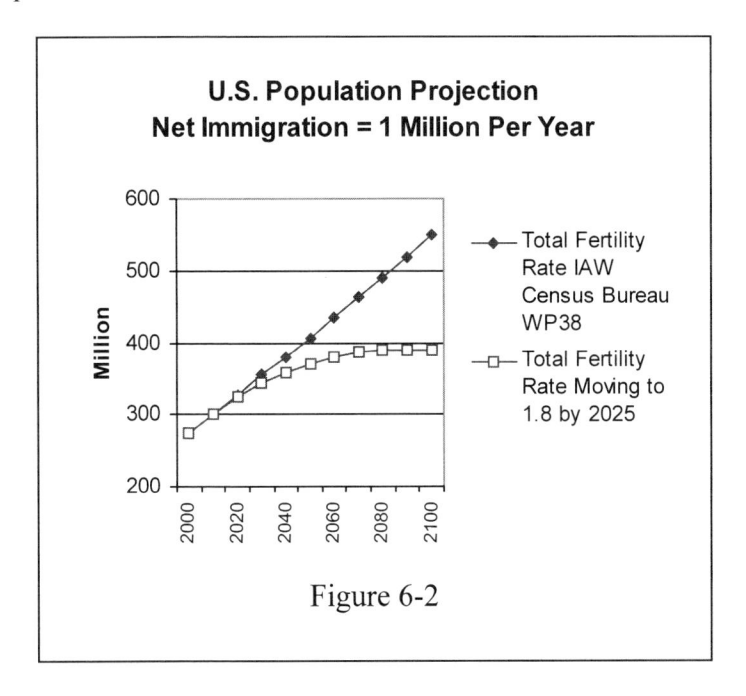

**U.S. Population Projection
Net Immigration = 1 Million Per Year**

- Total Fertility Rate IAW Census Bureau WP38
- Total Fertility Rate Moving to 1.8 by 2025

Figure 6-2

The Census Bureau's projection of U.S. total fertility rate tacitly assumes that there will be no effort to educate and influence fertility in a more beneficial direction. However, as we shall see shortly, there are a number of steps that can be taken that would not only influence fertility rate, but also provide other important societal benefits. With implementation of such steps, a TFR of 1.8 would not be overly difficult to achieve for three reasons.

First, we should be able to strive for this fertility reduction with racial and ethnic unity. The Census Bureau projects that all races (regardless of ethnic origin) will have a total fertility rate above 2.0 over most of this century (see Appendix B, Figure B-2). Therefore our efforts to reduce fertility must include *everyone* – regardless of race or ethnicity!

Second, in comparison to other developed nations, 1.8 is not a low rate, but one that is well above the modern norm: [144]

TFR	Country	Country	TFR
1.43	Japan	South Korea	1.65
1.72	Denmark	Finland	1.73
1.85	Norway	Sweden	1.57
1.72	United Kingdom	Greece	1.28
1.20	Italy	Spain	1.15
1.41	Austria	France	1.71
1.30	Germany	Switzerland	1.47

And third – the most important reason among the three – we know that well designed programs to influence fertility do work. We know that this is true because the Mexican Government has already achieved remarkable results. In the mid-70s, the average Mexican family had 7 children. Today the average is about 2.5. This amazing change in less than a generation is largely the result of government family planning officials who, since 1974, have implemented an enlightened state policy to reduce fertility. Mexico offers free family planning services, and Mexico's National Population Council promotes "small families" through advertising and entertainment programming on radio and television.[145]

Mexico's achievement stands in stark contrast to its southerly neighbor, Guatemala. Guatemala offers no state support for family planning, and Guatemala's fertility rate is nearly twice Mexico's.[146] Yet, even in countries that are averse to family planning, we can readily recognize a key to reducing fertility, i.e., education. In Guatemala the fertility rate of women with a secondary education is 2.7, roughly half Guatemala's overall rate.[147]

It is beyond the scope of this report to describe a specific program for reducing fertility in the U.S. But we can outline the major components of such a program:

- decrease the percent of U.S. youth who drop out of high school
- reduce poverty
- provide quality family planning services to women living in or near poverty, and
- use the immense educational potential of the media to influence the attitudes of all Americans in regard to child bearing.

Decreasing the Number of Dropouts

It is important to note that race and ethnicity are not the determinants of U.S. fertility that many people assume. Education level and the economic benefits associated with education are far more significant factors. Census Bureau data (Figure 6-3) show that fertility decreases dramatically with education – regardless of race and ethnicity.[148]

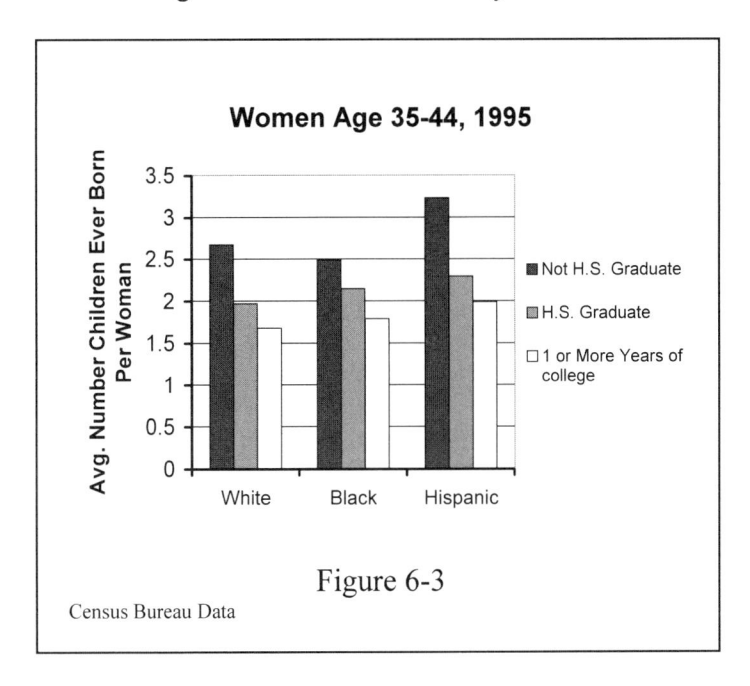

Figure 6-3

Census Bureau Data

Census Bureau data also show that as of 1999, 12% of our young adults (age 25 – 34) did not complete high school, and 43% had no college experience.[149] Both of these percentages are high; it is even a little shocking that nearly 1 in 8 of our young adults do not have a high school diploma. Given the scale of the numbers involved it is apparent that significantly reducing the high school dropout rate and increasing the number of our youth with at least one-year of college would significantly lower fertility. Moreover, in a high-technology society that demands an educated workforce, the multiple benefits of raising the number of people with at least some college experience are obvious.

Programs designed to reduce the high school dropout rate or increase the number of people with some college experience obviously require substantial funding. But taxes used to increase the education level of disadvantaged youth will benefit not only these youth, but our common future as well. When enough Americans understand this, the necessary funds will be allocated, and effective programs will be possible.

Reducing Poverty

It is well known that in our high-tech global economy, earning potential increases with educational achievement. Hence, we can infer from Figure 6-3 that women with low income have more children. Indeed, women with very low income give birth to about 50% more children (on a per capita basis) than women who are more financially secure (Figure 6-4).[150]

Why do low-income women have more children? According to Durning and Crowther, "They do so not because they are foolish or ignorant, as the common misconceptions hold. But because they are playing the hand they were dealt as best they can. Their entire life experience confirms they will not go far in the new, fiercely competitive global economy. They do not actively seek pregnancy, but they are less aggressive than women who are not poor in attempting to prevent it. They are less careful with contraception, and they accept [unintended] pregnancy when it happens. At least, they reason, they can be good mothers, raise good children, and fill their lives with the challenges and rewards of having a family. In a money-mad world, motherhood is one role they cannot be denied."[151] This explanation may be an oversimplification, but even so it captures a significant truth.

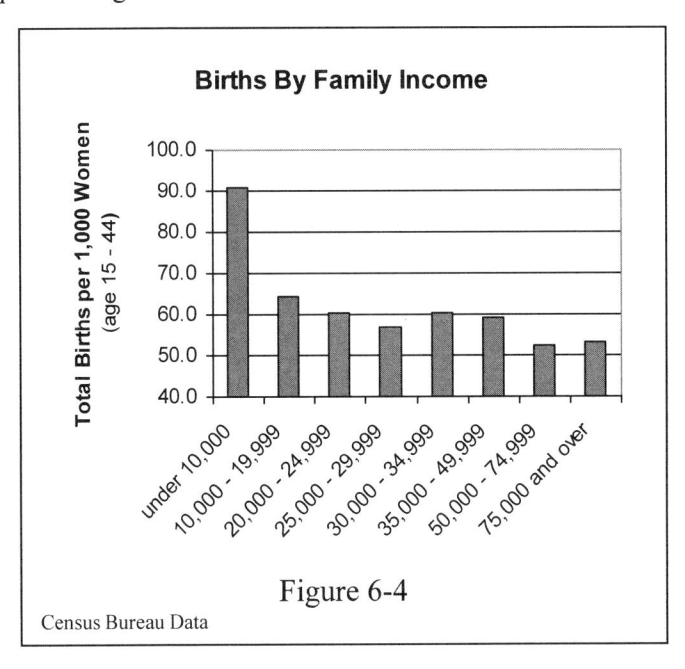

Births By Family Income

Figure 6-4

Census Bureau Data

Regardless of the reason, the statistics clearly show that in North America poverty increases fertility, and reducing poverty reduces the fertility rate:

- In 1972 the total fertility rate in the northwest states was around 2 children per woman, but in British Columbia the rate was only 1.6 children per woman. The reason is not that middle-class Americans wanted larger families than middle-class Canadians. It is that more Canadians are middle-class because Canadians are less willing to tolerate poverty in their society. Roughly one third of births in the

Pacific Northwest simply would not occur if the region eliminated poverty.[152]

- In 1996 the overall U.S. pregnancy rate was 9% lower than in 1990, and the teenage pregnancy rate was 15% lower than in 1990. One of three reasons cited for this is "the long economic expansion in the 1990's, increasing economic opportunity for teenagers as well as older women. Sexual activity of teenagers, for example, is closely associated with simple measures of economic prosperity. Economic opportunity may have given teenagers a reason to value more highly education and work. If appropriate services helped some teenagers to attain their new goals, this may help explain the declines in teenage pregnancy rates, as more teenagers were able to avoid early pregnancy and to attain their educational and occupational goals ..."[153]

In any given month approximately 25% of American children are living in poverty, and nearly 10% of American children live in chronic poverty.[154] The U.S. has the highest child poverty and the least effective safety net for children of any industrialized democracy.[155] Examples of child poverty rates in various affluent nations are provided in Figure 6-5.[156]

Thus, the United States has both the highest child poverty rate *and* the highest fertility rate of any industrialized democracy. This 'distinction' is surely a premier example of a "logical nexus" between social issues and environmental ends – a nexus that should unite people of many persuasions in collaborative action.[157]

Family Planning Services for Low-income Women

The history of attitudes toward family planning in the U.S. is mixed. Even as late as the 1960s, laws prohibiting counseling married couples about contraceptives were being enforced. It wasn't until 1965 that the U.S. Supreme Court (Griswold vs.

Connecticut) declared state laws prohibiting contraceptive use by married couples unconstitutional. It wasn't until the early '70s that low-income women were provided federal assistance (Title X services in 1970 and Medicaid family planning services in 1972). But by 1994, 3,119 agencies (e.g., health departments, Planned Parenthood affiliates, and hospitals) operated 7,122 publicly subsidized family planning clinics for an estimated 6.6 million women. These services prevent an estimated 1.3 million unintended pregnancies annually (and, as a consequence, result in 632,000 fewer abortions per year).[158]

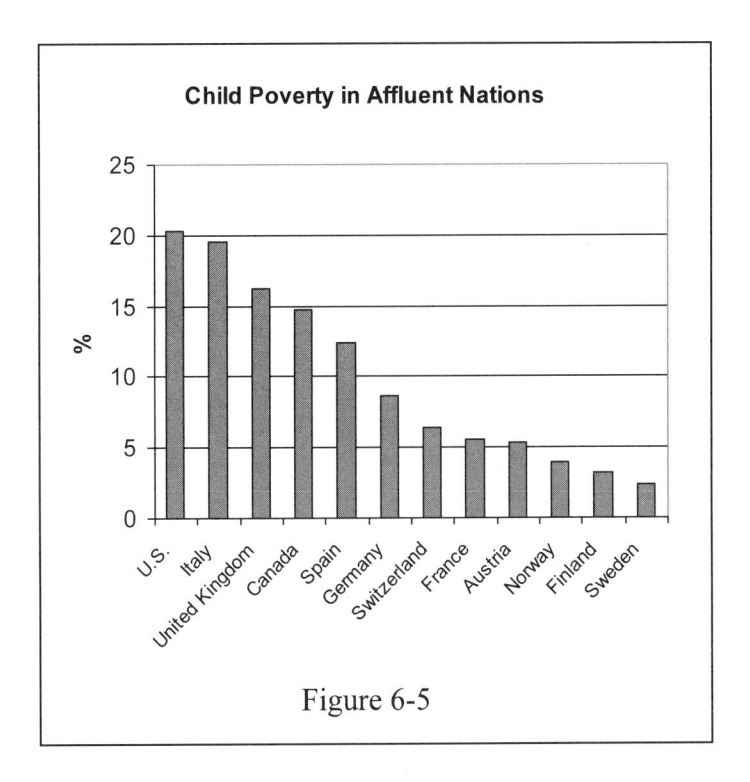

Child Poverty in Affluent Nations

Figure 6-5

While there is no doubt about the benefit of publicly subsidized family planning services, there is room for some improvement. Research shows that women's experiences with contraceptive and gynecologic providers affect both whether and how well women use contraceptives. Attention to the basics of courtesy and respect and, in the case of non-English speaking women, providing services in the client's language should be minimum criteria for service providers. In fact, studies provide strong evidence that treating clients well not only leads them to feel better about the services, but actually improves their chances of controlling their fertility. Unfortunately, improving services is likely to require more staff time and therefore greater expense, and increasing support for services to low-income women and men will be a challenge in an era of cost-containment.[159]

Rallying the political will for improved and expanded family planning services will not be easy. The difficulty lies not with lack of support from the majority of Americans. Indeed, in a recent national survey, Americans indicated overwhelming support for our federal government providing family planning services to poor women who want them, as part of their health care (Figure 6-6).[160]

The difficulty stems from groups outside the American mainstream that are working through the political process to impose their minority views on the rest of America. There are conservative religious organizations that oppose contraceptive use in general and public supported contraceptive use in particular. There are groups that appear to equate family planning with abortion, even though the overwhelming focus of family planning efforts is pregnancy prevention. And President Bush, seeking to court conservative religious groups, even tried to eliminate contraceptives from federal employees' health insurance coverage.[161]

Mr. Bush took his position even though:

1) 86% of Americans believe that health insurers should cover family planning services, as part of their regular health care coverage,[162]
2) fourteen states (beginning with Maryland in 1998) had already passed birth control equity laws – laws requiring

insurers to cover prescription contraceptives (incongruously, many insurers refusing to provide prescription contraceptive coverage leaped at the chance to provide anti-impotency prescription coverage), and
3) Mr. Bush probably knew that he would not have the support of the U.S. senate or the state legislators of his own home state of Texas.

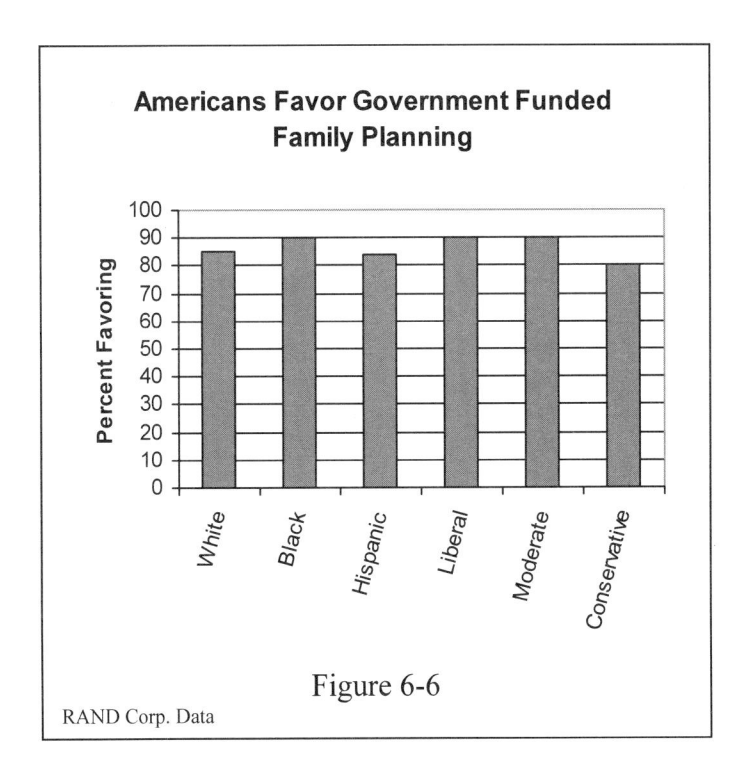

Americans Favor Government Funded Family Planning

Figure 6-6

RAND Corp. Data

Shortly after he took his position, fifty-three U.S. senators served notice that they would oppose his plan to kill contraceptive coverage, and Texas and Missouri joined the other fourteen states in enacting birth control equity laws.[163] Clearly, Mr. Bush's position gives ample testimony to the fact that conservative groups opposed to family planning are well organized, well financed, and wield political clout disproportionate to their numbers.

When family planning programs are debated, people concerned about the future of all Americans need to speak up. We need to remind everyone of the very real benefit that these programs provide, not only to the people who receive the assistance, but to our common future as well.

Educating and Influencing Attitudes

Attitudes formed by the prevailing culture and/or family history obviously have a lot to do with the number of children wanted by a couple. Attitudes also affect the number of unintended pregnancies. Research shows that ambivalence about sexuality can contribute to unintended pregnancy. More forthright acceptance of sexuality and help for couples to integrate their contraceptive use into their sexual relationship might therefore help reduce rates of unplanned births and abortions. While contraceptive service providers obviously have a role to play, there is a broader societal role as well. For example, salient public messages could well have a positive impact on method use.[164] In other words sexuality and contraception must be made normal subjects – not subjects that cause discomfort among many sexually active people.

Ideally this normalization would be the result of parental interaction. But in the real world additional approaches are required. Sex education in schools is an important approach, and well targeted media programs can also be highly influential. Mexico achieved its astounding success through both means. Sex education is mandatory in Mexican schools, and the Mexican media has been all but saturated with programs promoting the benefits of small families and the use of contraceptives.

In an article written for the *Sierra*, Mary Jo McConahay included the following to illustrate Mexico's sophisticated use of the media: "High above Mexico City's din, I found the Population Council's Secretary General Rodolfo Tuirán in his penthouse office, delighting in his latest television campaign, a series of mini-soap-opera ads in which two men argue about whether family planning is 'men's business' too. A grinning Tuirán bent forward from the sofa and quietly revealed how the series would end, a few months hence ...."[165]

Attitudes of adolescents regarding abstinence are also very important. The recent decline in teenage pregnancies has been linked to long term contraceptives, improved economic opportunities, and abstinence promotion programs. When so much of the entertainment and advertising industry is targeting youth with images of sexuality, and when nearly 1 in 14 women age 15 to 17 are becoming pregnant,[166] there is a clear need to counter the influence of much of the popular culture in the U.S.

There is a need to educate young people about responsible parenthood, and there is a need to educate young people about the consequences of continued population growth in the U.S. and the world.

Education of this sort is ongoing in the U.S. today. *Jam Packed* is an award-winning video produced for teens by Population Communications International (PCI). This 28-minute program introduces teenagers to the problems of rapid population growth and the effects of this growth on the environment. *MONICA EN BUSCA DE AMOR* (Monica in Search of Love) is a Spanish Language comic book that provides Latino teens with information about some of the common risks that adolescents face: dating violence, early pregnancy, and STDs. It is published by PCI in collaboration with a group of Latino teenagers and Gregory Molina, a Los Angles educator.

One of the most powerful tools for educating and influencing attitudes is television – particularly the soap operas. Each day 20 million U.S. viewers tune in at least one daytime soap opera. The potential value of the "soaps" to public health is so great that the U.S. Government is actively encouraging writers and producers to incorporate public health issues. At PCI's Soap Summit V, held in October 2000, every one of the ten daytime network soap operas was represented. The Summit featured the debut of the "Sentinel for Health Award for Daytime Drama." This award was created by the U.S. Centers for Disease Control and Prevention (CDC). Each year the award will recognize a soap opera for introducing a story line that accurately addresses an important public health concern.[167]

The CDC recognizes that the "soaps" have the power to influence behavior for the benefit of public health. Clearly the soaps and other mass media programming have the power to influence young people's behavior for a greater reduction in teen pregnancy, healthier newborns, and a lower fertility rate that will facilitate both a higher standard of living for many families and a stable U.S. population.

A Test of Our Progress

Discussions of efforts to stabilize population are often avoided because it is assumed that achieving stabilization will require some form of coercion or that the rights of some minority group will be abridged. Assumptions of this sort are entirely false. The unifying characteristics of the approaches just outlined are educating and helping – particularly helping those Americans who are not sharing in our great wealth.

Inscribed on a granite wall at the Franklin D. Roosevelt memorial in Washington is the following quote:

> *"The test of our progress is not whether we add more to the abundance of those who have much; it is whether we provide enough for those who have too little."*

We see now that aiding those who have too little is not simply an act of altruism; it is an act that will benefit our own children and grandchildren in a very tangible way. Conversely, failing to aid those who have too little will cause our children and grandchildren to suffer increasing quality of life declines – driven by continuing rapid population growth.

> *"When you hear talk about what to do with all the garbage, what to do about traffic, ... urban sprawl, ... almost any kind of people-related problem - sooner or later someone says that the real trouble is population growth. Everyone agrees; nothing can be done about population growth. That helpless response has always bothered me. People make populations grow. Surely people could make populations stop growing."*
>
> Donella Meadows, Adjunct Professor,
> Dartmouth College
> Co-author, "The Limits to Growth"
> LA Times, October 19, 1997

7

A Life-Changing Event

In writing *Earth Rising* (Island Press, 2000), New York Times writer Phillip Shabecoff interviewed more than 90 environmental leaders. During these interviews several acknowledged that they are winning battles but losing the war. These assessments were made in the context of looking back over progress since the first Earth Day 30 years ago.

In another 30 years the history of Smart Growth may also be chronicled as many battles won, but still losing the war – and the land.

In this report we have seen that Smart Growth cannot achieve the desired results if our mushrooming population is not reined in. We have seen that while there are people and organizations promoting population growth for their own financial gain, population growth is not necessary for the economic health of the nation. And we have seen that the U.S. population can be stabilized by means that the vast majority of Americans support, i.e., modestly reducing our fertility through entirely voluntary means.

Much of what is in this report is not new.

The essence of what we found in Chapter 2 is well known to every ecology student of the past thirty years. Whether we examine vanishing open space, worsening road congestion, escalating water worries, or factors impeding restoration of the Chesapeake Bay, we find that all of the problems are related to the interaction of population growth and per capita consumption of one form or another.

A Life-Changing Event

The interactions explained in Chapter 2 are not new insights; rather they are simply specific instances of the famous general relationship introduced by Ehrlich and Holdren in 1974:

$$I = P \times C$$

That is, adverse environmental impact (I) is equal to the population (P) times the per capita consumption (C) of that population.[168]

What this equation says is that vanishing open space, loss of wildlife habitat, depletion of fisheries, pollution in our waters, the vast majority of environmental and environmentally related quality of life issues, are driven by two factors: per capita consumption and the number of people. This simple relationship expresses a basic ecological law, a law just as immutable as the law of gravity:

> *In the long run, a society can continually grow its population and prevent further environmental degradation, if and only if each succeeding generation is willing to accept lower and lower levels of consumption.*

There may be a few technology enabled exceptions to this broad statement,[169] but a few exceptions will not grant us immunity.

Making the case for stabilizing our population is similarly not new. The need to stabilize the U.S. population has been understood at the highest levels of the U.S. government for decades:

- When the National Environmental Protection Act was signed into law by President Nixon, Title I of the act began: "The Congress, recognizing the profound impact of man's activity… particularly the profound influence of population growth…"

- *The Global 2000 Report to the President*, commissioned by Jimmy Carter recommended that "The United States should ... develop a U.S. national population policy that includes attention to issues such as population stabilization..."
- President Clinton's Council on Sustainable Development echoed its predecessors by declaring the need to "move toward stabilization of the U.S. population."[170]

Even our everyday experiences tell us that population growth is a primary cause of our environmental degradation and related quality of life concerns.

We all want our children and their descendents to enjoy a healthy environment, clean air and water, uncluttered land, ample open space, natural beauty, wilderness, and abundant wildlife. But in spite of presidential reports and everyday experiences, our population growth marches on – by far the highest population growth rate in the industrialized world.[171]

Why?

There is no simple answer to this question. However, an important piece of the answer lies in one of our culture's dominant stories: "Growth is Good." We hear this story repeated over and over again. We hear it told by politicians; we hear it told by business people and chambers of commerce; we see it in official government publications. We even hear it from people working hard to protect the environment. A particularly startling example from the environmental community is on the cover of the *Citizen's Guide to Shaping the Future of Maryland*. Included in large type is the subtitle: "Where do we GROW from here?"[172]

Of course some kinds of growth are good, and some are bad. Growth in per capita income for impoverished and low-income people is good. On the other hand, growth in carbon emissions from power plants and vehicles is bad. Growth in the crowds

A Life-Changing Event

at our favorite beach is bad. And as we have seen in this report, growth in population leads to massive sprawl, debilitating road congestion, and threats to our environment. But our culture's dominant story makes scant distinction. It simply insists – Growth is Good.

This story is so deeply imbedded in most of us – so persistently promoted by those who profit from it – that we are not even aware of it; we just act in consonance with it. To act in a more discerning manner we must be aware of the story; we must think about it and decide what is myth that enriches only a few, and what in the story is a truth that applies to all of us.

Actually recognizing the story and perceiving its true nature can be a life-changing event. In Daniel Quinn's novel, *Ishmael*, the main character, an unusual sage with a gift for discerning the human situation, explains this phenomenon to his student:

> "Once you learn to discern the voice of Mother Culture humming in the background, telling her story over and over again ...you'll never stop being conscious of it. Wherever you go for the rest of your life, you'll be tempted to say to the people around you, 'How can you listen to this stuff and not recognize it for what it is?'"[173]

Awareness precedes action. The number of people who recognize the "Growth is Good" story for what it is, the number of people who are aware of the population issues and solutions is a small but growing number. When enough people become aware, there will be a demand for change. There will be a demand for programs that promote population stabilization via voluntary means.

Until this change occurs, we, our children, and all future generations, will continue to experience declines in our environment and in our quality of life – despite the efforts of dedicated urban planners and environmentalists, despite all of our Smart Growth progress.

As stated earlier, the goal of this report is to increase awareness – to inform so as to help create a demand for change. The author and all who supported preparation of this report urge every reader to adopt the goal of increasing awareness. It is through our interaction with friends and associates, our letters to newspapers and public officials that the demand for change will occur.

Taking on a primary myth of our culture, challenging the Growth Machine, openly discussing why we must confront our mushrooming population, all will require patience and even some courage. But if our descendents are to enjoy the life that we wish for them, we must commit ourselves to speaking up.

This commitment is the essential life-changing event – the one that will matter to our children and grandchildren, and the generations that follow them.

Appendices

Appendix A – Growth Machine Organizations

Non-government Growth Machine Organizations

Maryland Chamber of Commerce The mission of the MCOC is to promote the ***growth***[174] and prosperity of its members.[175] Toward these ends the MCOC:
- coordinates lobbying activity with local chambers to stimulate economic development.
- works to improve the economic climate by reducing the over-regulation and the tax burden placed upon businesses.
- educates the business community regarding legislation, regulations, how the political arena operates, and how to become politically involved in state and local government.
- informs elected officials of the concerns of the business community

Prince George's Chamber of Commerce This COC operates through a variety of committees including:

Legislative Committee – The function of this committee is to "Aggressively promote pro-business legislation, and oppose legislation which threatens a healthy business climate at both state and local levels."

Economic Development Committee – The function of this committee is to "Improve the business climate for the expansion, retention, and ***attraction of business*** to Prince George's County, ..."[176]

Fairfax, VA Chamber of Commerce "The Fairfax County Chamber serves as a catalyst, leader and collaborator in efforts to promote pro-business, public policies at all levels of government."

"The Fairfax County Chamber's advocacy agenda covers a variety of issues affecting the business community, but places primary emphasis on improving transportation in our region, …, and supporting workforce training, *growth* and revitalization initiatives."

"As part of our advocacy efforts, the Fairfax County Chamber maintains full-time lobbyists on staff, participates in meetings of the Fairfax County Board of Supervisors, is active with local and regional transportation entities, works full-time in Richmond during each General Assembly session, maintains close working relationships with the members of Northern Virginia's Congressional delegation, and regularly testifies on Capitol Hill and at state and local governmental hearings."[177]

A major focus of the Fairfax COC is promoting roads and other transportation infrastructure. Within a week of John Kane's Techway e-mail to the BOT, David Guernsey, Chairman, Fairfax County Chamber of Commerce got a letter published in the *Washington Post* decrying the political setback that prompted Kane's e-mail.[178]

Greater Washington Board of Trade The BOT is an organization with interests and activities that range broadly. A primary interest is to "Better *Grow* the Region."[179] The BOT lobbies both federal and local governments in accomplishing its agenda. In June 2001 the BOT web site included the following among the descriptions of the various committees:

> *Government Affairs and Political Action Committees*: "Lobbies lawmakers on Capitol Hill, Virginia and Maryland state houses as well as the District of Columbia Council on issues ranging from work force development to transportation to tax credits for businesses. To help support and leverage lobbying

efforts, the Board of Trade has five political action committees:
- Federal PAC, ...
- CapNet, a federal technology PAC, ...
- VAPAC, ...
- MDPAC, ...
- DCPAC, ..."[180]

With 1,300 member corporations and more than 10,000 member executives, there is no better financed, local-issue lobbying group in the Washington area. Membership dues alone run from more than $500/year for firms with fewer than 50 employees to tens of thousands of dollars per year for corporations with thousands of employees in the region.

Government Growth Machine Organizations

Anne Arundel County "Our goal as county executives was to attract more economic development to our counties, so we zoned the land and developed the transportation plans 'needed' to accomplish that objective," James Lighthizer, former County Executive for Anne Arundel County, Maryland.[181]

Fairfax County Economic Development Authority The web site for the FCEDA explains the need as follows: "Residents typically use about $1.60 in public services for every dollar they contribute in taxes. On the other hand, businesses use about 40 cents in public services for every dollar they contribute in taxes. Recognizing this value of commercial development, the Fairfax County Board of Supervisors charged the county's Economic Development Authority (FCEDA) with *attracting more businesses* to the county." ... "By 2000 businesses contributed 25 percent of the real estate tax base, helping to pay for the high-quality public services – schools and social services, for example – that residents want. The number of Fairfax County residents is expected to top 1 million by 2003, and the population is increasingly diverse. The FCEDA *must continue to attract new businesses, workers and venture capital* to generate the business taxes that help pay for the services that residents will want and need."[182]

While the need for attracting businesses when Fairfax County was largely a bedroom community was straightforward, the current justification ignores the circular nature of the process. New businesses demand new workers; new workers and their families demand low cost services.

Montgomery County Department of Economic Development "The mission of the Department of Economic Development is to develop and implement strategies that will produce business and employment opportunities for residents of the County, *expand the County's economic base*, enhance the competitiveness of businesses located in the County, and promote the locational advantages of the County."[183]

Appendix B – Population Projection Information

Demographic Assumptions

The primary demographic assumptions used in making the projections of Figure 6-2 are as follows:

<u>Fertility Rates</u>: The actual fertility rates used are indicted in Figure B-1. The WP38 Middle Series fertility rates in Figure B-1 were downloaded from www.census.gov/population/www/projections/natdet.html. The ratio of males to females at birth was assumed to be 105 to 100.

Fertility Rates Used in Projections

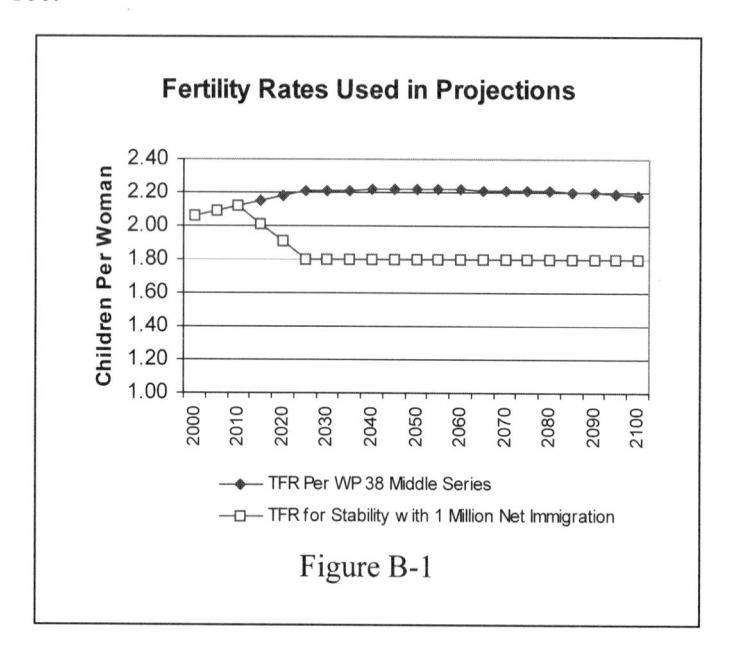

Figure B-1

Figure B-2 provides a summary version of TFRs including race/ethnic specific TFRs. Figure B-2 is included to show that all groups, regardless of race or ethnicity, will need to lower their TFR if we are to achieve a TFR of 1.8 for the country. In examining Figure B-2 one should remember the role that poverty and education play (see Chapter 6, Confronting Our National Population Growth).

The fertility rates in Figure B-2 are from "Methodology and Assumptions for the Population Projections of the United States, 1999 to 2100," Population Division Working Paper No. 38, U.S. Census Bureau, January 13, 2000, Table B.

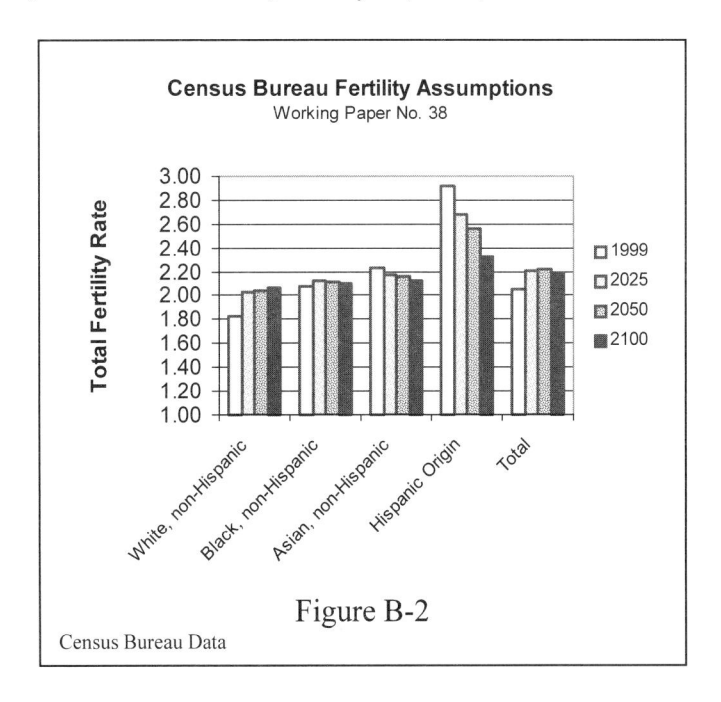

Census Bureau Fertility Assumptions
Working Paper No. 38

Figure B-2

Census Bureau Data

Life Expectancy: Table B-1 indicates the life expectancy projections used in the Census Bureau Working Paper 38, Middle Series projection. (Linear interpolation was used to obtain life expectancy at five year intervals since WP 38, Table C, provides data only for the years 1999, 2025, 2050, and 2100). Table B-1 also indicates the life expectancy projections used in generating Figure 6-2. There is a difference at year 2060 and beyond because the software program used to make the population projections in Figure 6-2 will not accept a life expectancy greater than 87.5 years.

Table B-1, Middle Series Life Expectancy

Year	Male	Female
2000	74.1	79.8
2005	74.8	80.6
2010	75.5	81.3
2015	76.2	82.1
2020	76.9	82.8
2025	77.6	83.6
2030	78.3	84.2
2035	79.0	84.8
2040	79.8	85.5
2045	80.5	86.1
2050	81.2	86.7
2055	81.9	87.3
2060	82.6	(87.5) 87.8
2065	83.2	(87.5) 88.4
2070	83.9	(87.5) 88.9
2075	84.6	(87.5) 89.5
2080	85.3	(87.5) 90.1
2085	86.0	(87.5) 90.6
2090	86.6	(87.5) 91.2
2095	87.3	(87.5) 91.7
2100	(87.5) 88.0	(87.5) 92.3

Net Immigration: Figure 6-2 is based on a net immigration of one million per year throughout the projection period. This is slightly higher than the 0.912 million to 0.984 million per year projections given in Table D (Middle Series), "Methodology and Assumptions for the Population Projections of the United States, 1999 to 2100," Population Division Working Paper No. 38, U.S. Census Bureau, January 13, 2000.

Throughout the projection period 46.3% of the immigrants are assumed to be male and 53.7% female. This distribution is that of the year 2000 Middle Series immigration projection used in Working Paper 38. The year 2000 was selected arbitrarily.

Other Assumptions: The initial population age distribution and the age distribution of immigrants are omitted from this Appendix. Both distributions were taken from the Year 2000 data provided with Working Paper 38. The more technical assumptions (e.g., age specific fertility) are also omitted from this Appendix.

Population Projection Software

The population projections provided in Figure 6-2 were produced using the "Spectrum Policy Modeling System," Version 1.55, a Windows based software program prepared as part of the Policy Project (The Futures Group International) with funding from the U.S. Agency for International Development. The software was downloaded from www.tfgi.com.

The software and the demographic data input to it were validated by duplicating the results of Working Paper 38 (Middle Series and Highest Migration Series). Agreement between Working Paper 38 and the Spectrum output were generally excellent. However, near the end of the projection period, differences of about 3% were noted. The primary reason for this divergence is presumed to be the inability of Spectrum to accept life expectancies greater than 87.5 years.

The objective in using this software was not to produce the best possible projections. Rather it was to produce projections that are in essence valid. A more elaborate effort would have produced "better" projections. But the degree of improvement would not have affected the thrust of the results presented in Figure 6-2.

Balancing Births, Deaths, and Net Immigration

To understand how the fertility rate and immigration level interact, note that the population change in any given year is given by:

Population Change = Births − Deaths + Net Immigration

To simplify matters we will ignore a factor called population momentum, and assume that average lifespan is unchanging. With these simplifications, the result of subtracting the number of deaths from the number of births will depend essentially on the total fertility rate (TFR). If the TFR is greater than 2.1, births will exceed deaths and population will increase each year. On the other hand if the TFR is less than 2.1, deaths will exceed births and, in the absence of a positive net immigration, the population will decrease each year. For the special case in which the amount by which deaths exceed births is equal to the net immigration, we have a stable population.

If a population maintains a TFR less than 2.1 but is still growing because of net immigration, the number by which deaths exceed births will grow each year. Ultimately, the number by which deaths exceed births will equal the net immigration (assuming a constant net immigration). Therefore, for any given TFR less than 2.1 and any given net immigration greater than zero, there is a corresponding population at which stability will be achieved.

But depending on specific parameter pairing, the size of the stable population can be either desirable or so enormous that the point of stability will have been lost almost entirely. For example, if the U.S. achieved and maintained a TFR of 1.8 but the net immigration rose to and remained at 2 million per year, stability would not be reached until the population of the U.S. approached 1 *billion* people!

Appendix C – Dependency Ratios

Historically, U.S. Social Security retirement benefits have not been funded by recipient and employer contributions made on behalf of the recipient. Rather, the benefits have been funded by contributions of those still in the work force. This system has worked well because the number of people of retirement age has been small compared to those of working age, and therefore the tax on working people to help fund current retiree benefits has been modest.

The measure of the number of persons of retirement age relative to those of working age is called the elder dependency ratio. This ratio is defined as the number of people 65 and older per hundred people ages 18 to 64 (or more recently 15 to 64). Figure C-1 depicts the dependency ratio over a hundred year period. The first 45% of the period is historical data; the latter 55% is that projected by the Census Bureau middle series.[184]

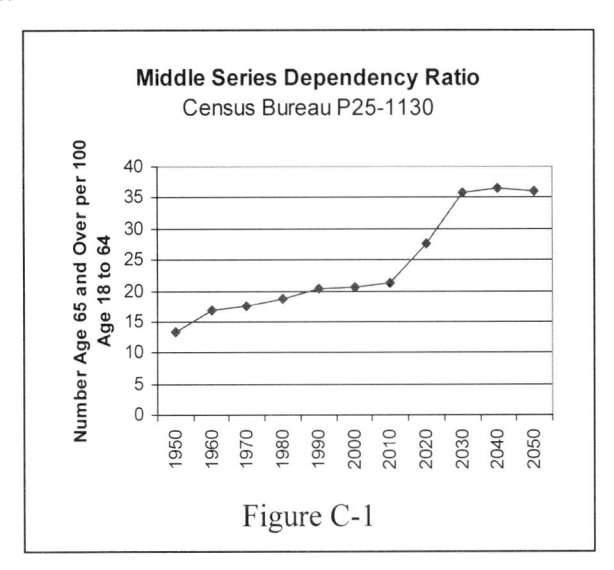

Figure C-1

The steep rise that begins after 2010 is primarily the result of the baby boom generation reaching retirement age. Or more precisely the steep rise is the result of the baby boomers reaching retirement age while all the 5-year cohorts following the baby boomers are smaller. (Reference Figure C-2, the baby boom generation causes the bulge in the population pyramid at the 5-year age cohorts near age 40.)

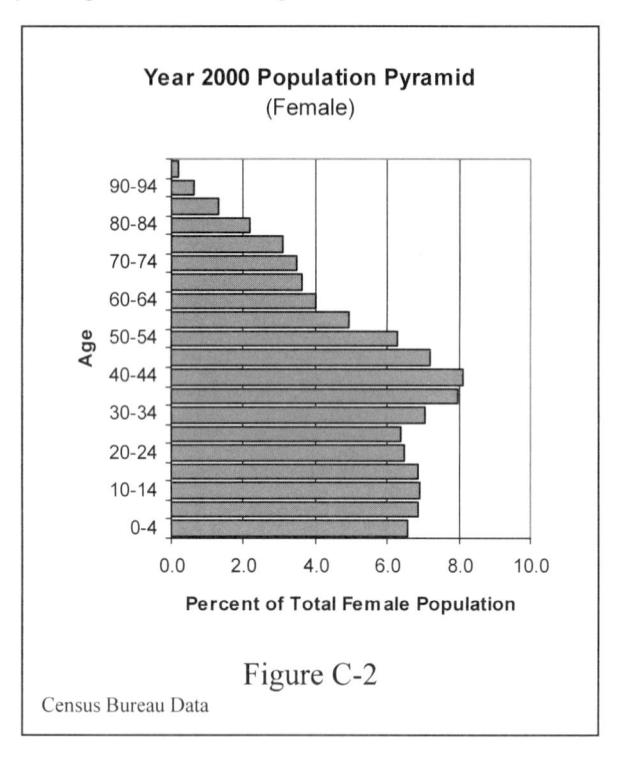

Figure C-2

Census Bureau Data

The relatively low dependency ratio prior to 2010 is due in large measure to the fact of the baby boomers being in the work force. That is, their presence makes it possible to operate the Social Security system at what may be regarded as an artificially low tax rate.

As we can see from Figure C-1, there are currently about 5 people of working age for each person of retirement age. But in another 30 years, the projection indicates that there will be slightly fewer than 3 people of working age for each person of retirement age. The impact of this change on funding Social Security benefits is the cause of much consternation among our politicians. After all, what politician wants to tell his/her constituents that either taxes must go up or benefits must go down.

Looking at Figure C-2, it is logical to ask if we could keep our dependency ratio from climbing by increasing immigration. The United Nations Population Division investigated this question and concluded that in order to maintain the current dependency ratio, the level of immigration required would be so great that by the year 2050 the U.S. population would exceed *1 billion* people![185] Not surprisingly, the UN Report observes that, for the U.S., "immigration is not a realistic solution to demographic aging."[186]

In making projections out to the year 2100, the Census Bureau provides three dependency ratios, corresponding to their lowest migration, middle, and highest migration population projection series (Figure C-3).[187] As we can see from the figure, the Census Bureau reaches the same conclusion as the United Nations Population Division: the U.S. dependency ratio is going to soar well above its Year 2000 level. Also, by noting the differences among the three series, we can readily see that even enormous differences in year 2100 population have relatively negligible effect on the dependency ratio.

What is the elder dependency ratio in a stable population? The answer depends on two factors: the mean longevity (life expectancy) of the population, and the accepted retirement age. Figure C-4 illustrates how the dependency ratio changes as these factors change.[188] What the figure reveals is readily supported by our intuition. As our lifespan increases it is obvious that the number of "elder" people will increase. Similarly, it is obvious that we can reduce the number of elder dependents by raising the age at which retirement benefits are awarded.

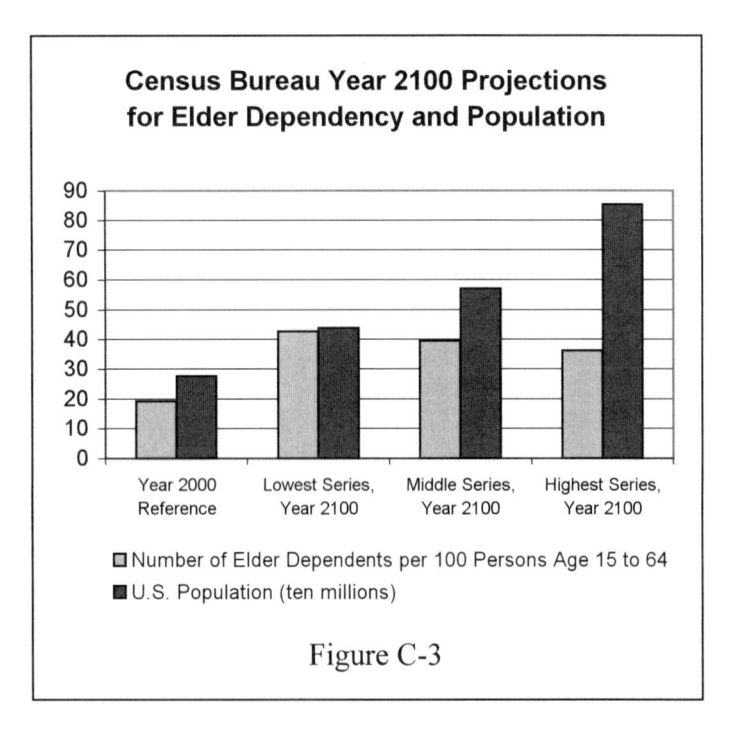

Census Bureau Year 2100 Projections for Elder Dependency and Population

[Bar chart showing four categories: Year 2000 Reference (~20, ~28); Lowest Series, Year 2100 (~43, ~44); Middle Series, Year 2100 (~40, ~57); Highest Series, Year 2100 (~37, ~85). Legend: Number of Elder Dependents per 100 Persons Age 15 to 64; U.S. Population (ten millions).]

Figure C-3

If for a given longevity and retirement age, a dependency ratio lower than that indicated in Figure C-4 becomes a policy objective, the only way to achieve it will be to increase the working age population. But by doing so, we will put ourselves into a trap. The added working age people will soon reach retirement, and swell the ranks of the elder dependents even more. Consequently we are again confronted with the need to add even more people to the working age population in order to maintain the low dependency ratio.

The essential point is that for any given longevity and retirement age in Figure C-4, it is impossible to achieve and sustain a lower dependency ratio without committing the U.S. to a population that forever grows larger and larger. But it is

Appendix C

also physically impossible for our population to grow forever. Therefore any policy that increases our working age population in order to reduce the dependency ratio is a self-serving policy that only shifts the day of reckoning to a future generation.

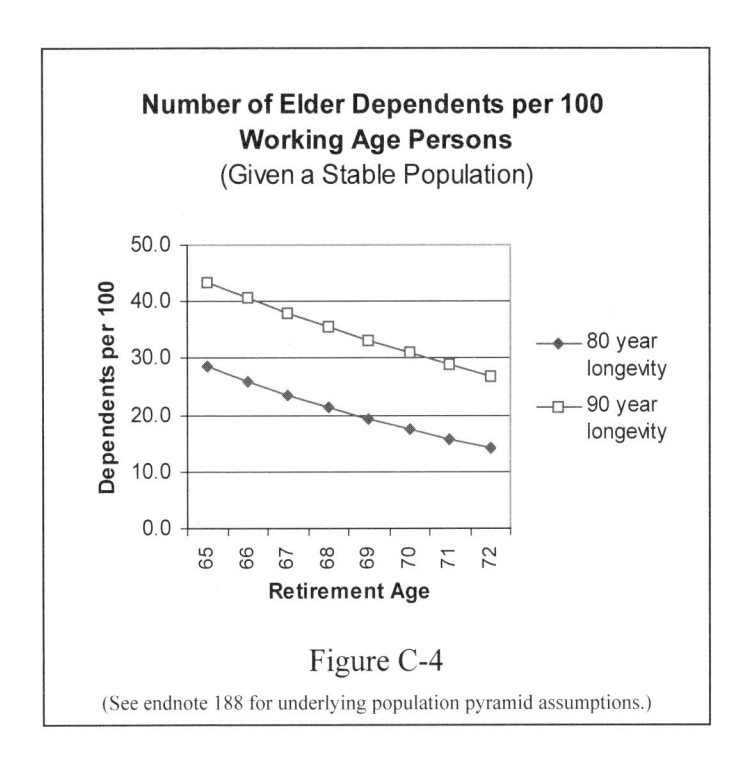

Number of Elder Dependents per 100 Working Age Persons
(Given a Stable Population)

Figure C-4

(See endnote 188 for underlying population pyramid assumptions.)

Appendix D – Declining Per Capita VMT Growth

This appendix discusses a subject judged too specialized for inclusion in the body of the report. It is included here because the quantitative information provided is important for readers especially interested in the road congestion issue.

Per Capita VMT Growth: Figures 2-3 and 2-4 show the projected Washington Area Per Capita VMT growth for the period 2000 – 2025 to be only about one fourth the growth for the period 1982 – 1999. To help understand why such a dramatic reduction in growth could be possible, we will examine the components of Per Capita VMT growth as provided in the 1995 Nationwide Personal Transportation Survey for the period 1983 to 1995 (Figure D-1).[189]

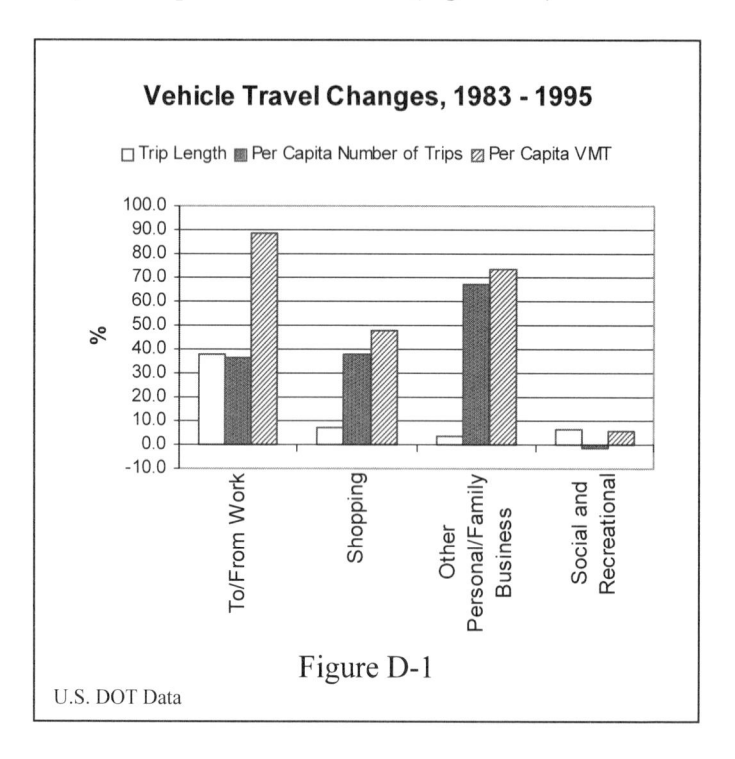

Figure D-1

U.S. DOT Data

It is often asserted that our growth in per capita VMT is a consequence of sprawl. Such assertions are an over-simplification. The survey data in Figure D-1 shows that in the three travel categories experiencing significant per capita VMT growth, increased numbers of vehicle trips is largely responsible for the growth in per capita VMT. Further, additional survey data strongly suggests that most of the increase in per capita trips is due, not to sprawl, but to personal choice.

The category "Personal/Family Business" includes trips for the purchase of *services* (banking, legal, haircuts, dry cleaning, exercise clubs, auto repair, pet grooming, etc.). The increase in per capita VMT for this category was almost entirely due to increased per capita trips. The average trip distance (around 7 miles) barely changed. In 1995 the per capita number of trips for this category was 238 – astoundingly, almost five trips per week.

The increase in per capita VMT for "Shopping" also was almost entirely due to increased per capita trips. Again, the average trip distance (around 5.5 miles) barely changed. In 1995 the per capita number of shopping trips was 190 – almost four trips per week.

Since the average trip distances for both Shopping and Personal/Family Business changed little, and exceeds the distance that people routinely walk, it is difficult to believe that many people are making more vehicle trips because they must now drive where they previously walked.

Similarly it is difficult to believe that many people are making more vehicle trips because they no longer have access to mass transit. This line of reasoning is supported by comparing the increase in person trips (including walking and transit) with the increase in vehicle trips (Figure D-2).[190]

For the data used in Figure D-2, a trip is a distance of more than four blocks.[191] At such a small distance it is unlikely that city or inner suburb residents can accomplish more in a single trip than residents of the outer suburbs. Therefore we may reasonably conclude that the increase in person trips is primarily the result of personal choice, and not related significantly to place of residence. And since the increase in vehicle trips is little different from the increase in person trips, the same can be said of the increase in vehicle trips.

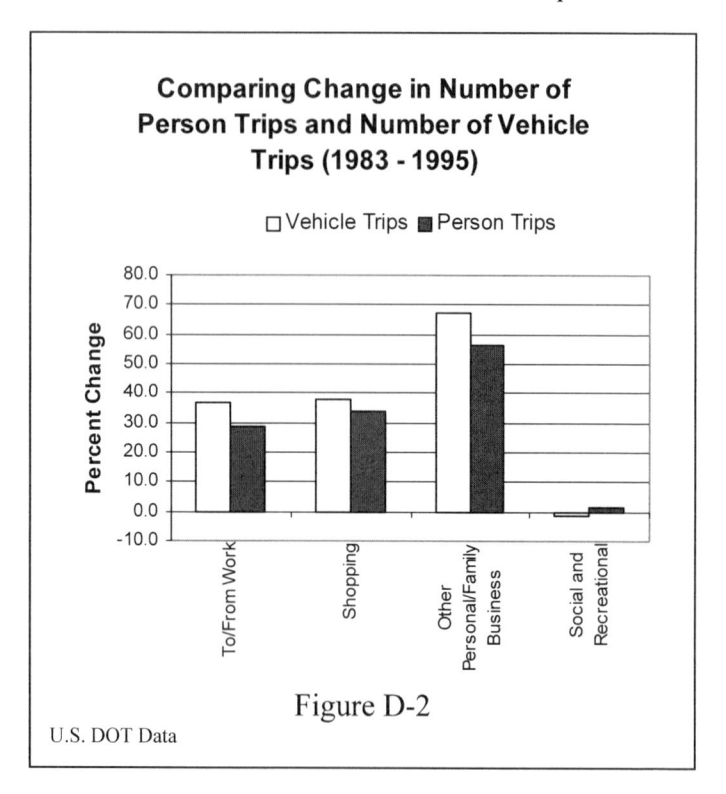

Comparing Change in Number of Person Trips and Number of Vehicle Trips (1983 - 1995)

□ Vehicle Trips ■ Person Trips

Figure D-2

U.S. DOT Data

The Per Capita VMT for the category "To/From Work" increased the most, and the increase was due to both the number of trips and the trip distance. The increase in trip distance is clearly related to sprawl. As the population of the area grows and as we spread out looking for attractive

Appendix D

affordable housing, the distance from home to work obviously increases. We can try to work close to where we live, but with two income households and frequent job changes, achieving this objective is difficult.

The increased number of per capita to/from work trips has two obvious reasons. First, part of the increase in the number of trips is due to an increase in the number of workers per capita. Between 1983 and 1995, the per capita number of workers increased by roughly 13%.[192]

The second obvious reason for the increase in the number of trips is the decrease in carpooling. Nationwide, between 1983 and 1995, carpooling decreased nearly 12%.[193] (Average To/From Work occupancy went from 1.29 to 1.14 persons per vehicle.) The combined impact of 13% more per capita workers and 12% less carpooling results in a 28% increase in the To/From Work trips per capita. In other words, well over half of the reported increase in per capita To/From Work trips is accounted for by changes in workforce participation and carpooling habits.

The preceding discussion of national trends does not validate COG's projection of 11% per capita VMT growth for the Washington area (depicted in Figure 2-8). But if we assume that the Washington area travel statistics are similar to the national statistics, COG's projection of slowing per capita growth should not surprise us. After all, most of the prior increase in per capita workers was due to women entering the workforce. And given the current substantial fraction of women in the workforce, we should expect future increases to be smaller. Similarly, there are limits to the amount of time people are willing to give to purchasing goods and services. Again, we should expect future increases in the per capita number of trips for these purposes to be smaller.

Endnotes

[1] In the fifteen years preceding 1997, the population of the Portland area grew 32%; "Who Sprawls Most," William Fulton, Rolf Pendall, Mai, Nguyen, and Allicia Harrison, Brookings Institution, July 2001
[2] "The future is in our hands," *The Willamette Chronicle*, paid supplement, April 2001.
[3] "Urban Sprawl," National Geographic Magazine, July 2001, page 71
[4] "A Complex Relationship: Population Growth and Suburban Sprawl," Summer 2001, www.sierraclub.org/sprawl/population.asp; earlier in 2001, a proposal to require the Club to "emphasize both regional and national population stabilization as essential components in all Sierra Club sprawl materials and programs," was narrowly defeated in a nation-wide referendum.
[5] *Holding Our Ground*, Tom Daniels and Deborah Bowers, Island Press, 1997, pp. 146 and 180
[6] Using the INS estimate of 275,000 illegal immigrants per year, gross immigration over the period 1995 – 1998 ranged from 935,000 to 1,190,000. Using the INS estimate of 222,000 emigrants per year, it is seen that over the same period, net immigration ranged from 713,000 to 968,000. Sources: "Legal Immigration, Fiscal Year 1998" Immigration and Naturalization Service, May 1999; "1998 Statistics Yearbook of Immigration and Naturalization," Immigration and Naturalization Service. http://www.ins.usdoj.gov/graphics/aboutins/statistics/Emigrat.htm
[7] See Chapter 6, "Confronting Our National Population Growth."
[8] "Concern Over Population Growth Among Americans Less Prevalent Now Than In Past," Gallup News Service, September 1999
[9] "As the Economy Grows, the Trees Fall", Glenn Frankel and Stephen Fehr, The Washington Post, March 23, 1997.
[10] *Land and the Chesapeake Bay*, Chesapeake Bay Foundation, © 2000, p1
[11] On behalf of The Wilderness Society and other land conservation organizations, the Mellman Group, Inc. designed and administered a telephone survey between November 14-17, 2000 of 600 adults residing within the Potomac River watershed region, including 300 within the Washington metro area and 300 outside the Washington metro portion of the watershed.
[12] Poll results published January 9, 2001 in the *Baltimore Sun*

Endnotes 125

[13] "We Caused Sprawl Ourselves", David Olinger, *The Denver Post*, February 7, 1999.
[14] Sierra Club 1999 Sprawl Report, Chapter 2.
[15] *Growth at the Ballot Box*, Brookings Institution, February 2001.
[16] Results from "Advanced Search" at washingtonpost.com. Search performed March 7, 2001
[17] Brown fields or other developed but abandoned properties are not considered open space.
[18] "Who Sprawls Most?," W. Fulton, R. Pendall, M. Nguyen, and A. Harrison, Brookings Institution, July 2001
[19] Starting with $A = P \times U$ and allowing both population and per capita land consumption to grow by amounts ΔP and ΔU, the following can be readily derived: $\Delta A/A = \Delta P/P + \Delta U/U + (\Delta P/P)(\Delta U/U)$. The first right hand term is the blame attributed to population growth; the second is the blame attributed to the increase in per capital land consumption, and the third is attributed to "uncertain" because both factors are involved, and there is no totally satisfactory way of separating them.
[20] *Weighing Sprawl Factors in Large U.S. Cities*, Kolankiewicz and Beck, March 19, 2001, Appendix A
[21] See Chapter 3, Growth Pressures, for the definition of the extended Washington area, and the details behind the projected increase in population.
[22] "Who Sprawls Most?," W. Fulton, R. Pendall, M. Nguyen, and A. Harrison, Brookings Institution, July 2001, Appendix B
[23] Denver's 1990 urban area was 459 square miles. *Weighing Sprawl Factors in Large U.S. Cities*, Kolankiewicz and Beck, March 19, 2001, Appendix B
[24] "Who Sprawls Most?," W. Fulton, R. Pendall, M. Nguyen, and A. Harrison, Brookings Institution, July 2001, Table 2
[25] 1997 density of the area was 8.31 persons per urban acre. "Who Sprawls Most?," W. Fulton, R. Pendall, M. Nguyen, and A. Harrison, Brookings Institution, July 2001, Table 2
[26] "Answers to Maryland Poll Questions," *Baltimore Sun*, January 9, 2001
[27] "The 2001 Urban Mobility Report," Table A-2, Texas Transportation Institute, http://mobility.tamu.edu/2001/study/cities/tables/washington_dc.pdf

[28] "The Mobility Data for Washington, DC-MD-VA," part of "The 2001 Urban Mobility Report by the Texas Transportation Institute. http://mobility.tamu.edu/2001/study/cities/tables/washington_dc.pdf

[29] "The Mobility Data for Washington, DC-MD-VA," part of "The 2001 Urban Mobility Report by the Texas Transportation Institute. http://mobility.tamu.edu/2001/study/cities/tables/washington_dc.pdf (Between 1982 and 1999, VMT on the Washington roadway system increased 82%)

[30] "Facts About the 2000 Constrained Long Range Plan," Metropolitan Washington Council of Governments (The VMT increase is projected to be a comparatively modest 46%.)

[31] Appendix D provides additional information regarding per capita VMT growth, including a rationale for the slowing of per capita VMT growth.

[32] The 2001 Urban Mobility Report, Texas Transportation Institute, May 2001, Exhibit 6

[33] "Study Backs More Spending on Transit," *The Washington Post*, December 19, 1999

[34] *The 2001 Urban Mobility Report*, Texas Transportation Institute, page iii

[35] "Why I Changed My Mind On a New River Crossing," by Representative Frank Wolf, a letter published in *The Washington Post* on June 3, 2001.

[36] "Bad Traffic Grows Worse Study Says," *The Washington Post*, December 16, 1999

[37] "Induced Travel: Definition, Forecasting Process, And a Case Study in the Metropolitan Washington Region," National Capital Region Transportation Planning Board Metropolitan Washington Council of Governments, September 19, 2001

[38] Summary of Travel Trends 1995 Nationwide Personal Transportation Survey, December 1999, USDOT

[39] "Crowded Metro Looks at Short-Term Fixes," *Washington Post*, September 28, 2001

[40] "Mass Transit Popularity Surges in U.S.," *Washington Post,* Sunday, April 30, 2000; Page A01

[41] *1997 Update to the Financially Constrained Long-Range Transportation Plan*, Metropolitan Washington Council of Governments, Table 5-1

[42] "Transit Service Expansion Plan," Washington Metropolitan Area Transit Authority, April 1999, p8

Endnotes 127

[43] See Chapter 3, chapter titled "Washington Area Population Growth" for definition of Washington Metropolitan Statistical Area and the Extended Washington Area. County areas are from "Land Area, Population, and Density for States and Counties: 1990," US Census Bureau, Released: March 12, 1996.

[44] Figure constructed using American Fact Finder, a mapping tool available at www.census.gov. (Click on American FactFinder and then on Reference Maps.)

[45] *National Strategic Transportation Planning Study – Washington Metropolitan Area*, Executive Summary, September 1999, Table 6

[46] *Office Sprawl: The Evolving Geography of Business*, Brookings Institution, November 2000

[47] *Office Sprawl: The Evolving Geography of Business*, Brookings Institution, November 2000

[48] "Transit Service Expansion Plan," Washington Metropolitan Area Transit Authority, April 1999, pp10,11.

[49] "Transportation Policy Task Force Report," To Montgomery County [MD] Planning Board, January 17, 2002, Figure 3.5

[50] "Facts About the 2000 CLRP," Metropolitan Washington Council of Governments, http://www.mwcog.org/trans/clrplist.htm

[51] "1997 Update to the Financially Constrained Long-Range Transportation Plan," Transportation Planning Board, Metropolitan Washington Council of Governments, Table 5-1

[52] "Water-Use Worries in Clarksburg, Golf Course Plan Heightens Concern," Fern Shen, *Washington Post*, July 11, 1999.

[53] "Water-Use Worries in Clarksburg, Golf Course Plan Heightens Concern," Fern Shen, *Washington Post*, July 11, 1999.

[54] "Washing Cars, filling Pools could bring Sanctions," Michael Shear, Daniel LeDuc, *Washington Post*, August 5, 1999.

[55] "Drought Declared in Central Md.," David Snyder, *Washington Post*, April 6, 2002

[56] 'We're Missing the Bigger Picture," Bill Matuszeski, *Washington Post*, April 21, 2002

[57] League of Women Voters of the National Capital Area, Water Supply Task Force, February 1999, *Drinking Water Supply in the Washington, D.C. Metropolitan Area: Prospects and Options for the 21st Century*. (Washington, D.C.: League of Women Voters of the National Capital Area), page iv.

[58] *Year 2000 Twenty-Year Water Demand Forecast*, Interstate Commission for the Potomac River Basin, October 2000, Appendix L

[59] Projected average use, 1930 drought flow, and 1966 drought flow data are from League of Women Voters of the National Capital Area, Water Supply Task Force, February 1999, *Drinking Water Supply in the Washington, D.C. Metropolitan Area: Prospects and Options for the 21st Century*. (Washington, D.C.: League of Women Voters of the National Capital Area), Table 3 and page 1 respectively. Normal flow (not shown) for the months of September and October is about 1.8 billion gallons per day; ref. USGS, http://md.usgs.gov/monthly/potwash/Report_1999_10.html and http://md.usgs.gov/monthly/potwash/Report_1999_9.html

[60] The "demand" may be understated if we consider the needs of aquatic life. As depicted in the figure, the demand includes 100 million gallons of water per day of "flowby" – the minimum amount of water to be left in the Potomac to support aquatic life. This minimum amount has been criticized as being inadequate, and future studies may indicate a larger minimum flowby. Indeed, in a letter published in the *Washington Post*, ("Stream of Environmental Consciousness," August 21, 1999) Michael Nelson noted that at the time the 100 mgd flowby was established by the Maryland Department of Natural Resources, the U.S. Fish and Wildlife Service recommended a flowby between 800 million and 1,200 million gallons per day.

[61] League of Women Voters of the National Capital Area, Water Supply Task Force, February 1999, *Drinking Water Supply in the Washington, D.C. Metropolitan Area: Prospects and Options for the 21st Century*. (Washington, D.C.: League of Women Voters of the National Capital Area), page 19.

[62] Ibid.

[63] Ibid.

[64] *Year 2000 Twenty-Year Water Demand Forecast*, Interstate Commission for the Potomac River Basin, October 2000, page 4-8

[65] League of Women Voters of the National Capital Area, Water Supply Task Force, February 1999, *Drinking Water Supply in the Washington, D.C. Metropolitan Area: Prospects and Options for the 21st Century*. (Washington, D.C.: League of Women Voters of the National Capital Area), page 11.

[66] League of Women Voters of the National Capital Area, Water Supply Task Force, February 1999, *Drinking Water Supply in the Washington, D.C. Metropolitan Area: Prospects and Options for the

21st Century. (Washington, D.C.: League of Women Voters of the National Capital Area), page 19.
[67] Ibid., page 20.
[68] League of Women Voters of the National Capital Area, Water Supply Task Force, February 1999, *Drinking Water Supply in the Washington, D.C. Metropolitan Area: Prospects and Options for the 21st Century*. (Washington, D.C.: League of Women Voters of the National Capital Area), page 26
[69] Ibid., page 27
[70] *Our Stolen Future*, Coburn, Dumanoski, and Myers, Plume Books, 1997, pages 137 , 138
[71] "Drug Wastes Pollute Waterways," Eric Pianin, *Washington Post*, March 13, 2002.
[72] Preceding four paragraphs were excerpted from *Our Stolen Future*, Coburn, Dumanoski, and Myers, Plume Books, 1997, pages 131 - 134
[73] *Our Stolen Future*, Coburn, Dumanoski, and Myers, Plume Books, 1997, page 141
[74] League of Women Voters of the National Capital Area, Water Supply Task Force, February 1999, *Drinking Water Supply in the Washington, D.C. Metropolitan Area: Prospects and Options for the 21st Century*. (Washington, D.C.: League of Women Voters of the National Capital Area), pages 27, 28
[75] For example, an increase by a factor of ten would result for the case in which the dilution is 33% (one part natural river water to two parts effluent), treatment at Blue Plains removes 33% of the chemicals, and the concentration of chemicals in the naturally flowing Potomac is 10% of the concentration in the usual Blue Plains effluent. (Calculation by author.)
[76] "Down in the Dead Zone", Peter Annin, *Newsweek*, October 1999
[77] Mr. Boesch's comments excerpted from "Tangle of Trouble Stifles Life in Bay," Heather Dewar, *The Baltimore Sun*, June 13, 1999
[78] Chesapeake Bay Program, PowerPoint Presentation, Environmental Indicators, Track 2 - Living Resource Indicator, 6/27/01, speaker notes, slide 1, Acres of Bay Grasses
[79] Chesapeake Bay Program, PowerPoint Presentation, Environmental Indicators, Track 2 - Living Resource Indicator, 6/27/01, speaker notes, Acres of Bay Grasses slide

[80] Chesapeake Bay Program, PowerPoint Presentation, Environmental Indicators, Track 2 - Living Resource Indicator, 6/27/01, Acres of Bay Grasses slide

[81] 1985 data, Chesapeake Bay Program, PowerPoint Presentation, Environmental Indicators, Measuring Our Progress, 8/8/01, speaker notes, sources of Nutrient Loads to the Bay slide. Note: the nitrogen falling to land is included in the percentages for agriculture, forest, and septic systems.

[82] Chesapeake Bay Program, PowerPoint Presentation, Environmental Indicators, Track 4 – Cross Cutting Indicators, 8/22/01

[83] Chesapeake Bay Program, PowerPoint Presentation, Environmental Indicators, Track 4 – Cross Cutting Indicators, 8/22/01, speaker notes.

[84] Chesapeake Bay Program, PowerPoint Presentation, Environmental Indicators, Track 4 – Cross Cutting Indicators, 8/22/01, Municipal Nitrogen Discharge and Population slide (slide 19)

[85] Chesapeake Bay Program, PowerPoint Presentation, Environmental Indicators, Track 4 – Cross Cutting Indicators, 8/22/01, Municipal Nitrogen Discharge and Population slide

[86] It is worthwhile to note that the per capita nitrogen discharged from a municipal plant is independent of the extent to which Smart Growth is implemented in the area served by the plant. As density little affects the per capita water consumption, it little affects the per capita sewage that we produce.

[87] Chesapeake Bay Program, PowerPoint Presentation, Environmental Indicators, Measuring Our Progress, 8/8/01, Sources of Nutrient Loads to the Bay slide.

[88] *Land and the Chesapeake Bay*, Chesapeake Bay Foundation, June, 2000, page 15

[89] *Holding Our Ground*, Tom Daniels and Deborah Bowers, Island Press 1997, page 251

[90] Original quote in the *Oregonian*, April 7, 1998; cited in "Endless Growth or the End of Growth," Andy Kerr, President of Alternatives to Growth Oregon, September 2000

[91] The two counties are often included when the Washington area is discussed. For example, they are included by the Metropolitan Washington Council of Governments, "Cooperative Forecasting: Round 6 Technical Report," January 1999.

[92] *Cooperative Forecasting: Round 6 Technical Report, January 1999*, Metropolitan Council of Governments, p 29. Note: COG

Endnotes 131

projections are for 2020; linear extrapolation was used to extend them to 2025.

[93] *Methodology and Assumptions for the Population Projections of the United States: 1999 – 2100*, Population Division Working Paper Number 38, U.S. Census Bureau, January 13, 2000

[94] "2100 Census Forecast: 2000 x 2," By D'Vera Cohn, *Washington Post*, January 13, 2000

[95] Belgium, Netherlands and Switzerland have land areas comparable to the land are of Maryland. Ireland, Austria and Portugal have land areas about three times that of Maryland. And the land area of the United Kingdom is about ten times that of Maryland. (Regarding Mr. Hollmann's comparison, note that the land area of the United States is nearly forty times that of the United Kingdom.)

[96] The densities provided in the figure are based on land areas taken form the *World Book* encyclopedia, and population estimates and projections taken from "The State of the World Population 1999," United Nations Population Fund, and the Population Reference Bureau projections for 2025 and 2050. The PRB data was obtained from http://www.prb.org/Content/NavigationMenu/Other_reports/2000-2002/sheet2.html

[97] 582.6 million. *World Book Encyclopedia*, 1974

[98] The key data points from which this conclusion is drawn are as follows: 1) 2100 middle series projection of 571 million people, 2) the 2100 zero migration projection of 377 million, and a total net immigration of 93 million. Reference: *Methodology and Assumptions for the Population Projections of the United States: 1999 – 2100*, Population Division Working Paper Number 38, U.S. Census Bureau, January 13, 2000. It may be of further interest to note that due to our current demographic momentum, the zero migration case population growth could be avoided only by reducing the total fertility rate below replacement level (2.1).

[99] *Methodology and Assumptions for the Population Projections of the United States: 1999 – 2100*, Population Division Working Paper Number 38, U.S. Census Bureau, January 13, 2000

[100] Quote found in http://www.flsuspop.org/docs/NPG/NPGMissed.htm

[101] "Sprawl, Traffic Congestion, and the Box that Bars Relief," Edwin Stennett, *Montgomery Sierran*, June 2000

[102] *Statistical Abstracts of the United States 1992*, Table 614 and *Statistical Abstracts of the United States 2000*, Table 649. For similar results over earlier time intervals see "The City as Growth Machine," by Harvey Molotch, in the *American Journal of Sociology*, 1976.

[103] "Officials Base Subsidies On Flawed Model," Jay Hancock, *The Baltimore Sun*, October 12, 1999.

[104] *Better, Not Bigger*, Eben Fodor, 1999, page 64

[105] Many people first heard the phrase "In Growth We Trust" from Professor Albert Bartlett, University of Colorado. But Professor Bartlett declines attribution – indicating that he does not recall coining the phrase, nor does he remember where he first heard it. (personal correspondence)

[106] "Growth Without Growth," Paul D. Gottlieb, Brookings Institution, February 2002. The study author points out that if the data points for Austin Texas (the upper most point in the diagram) and Las Vegas, Nevada (the right most point) were removed, what little relationship between population growth and per capita economic growth suggested by the trendline would disappear.

[107] *Statistical Abstracts of the United States* (1992 and 2000), Census Bureau, Tables 1375 (1992) and 1352 and 1365 (2000)

[108] Statement made August 5, 2001. Quote taken from "Alexander's Gas and Oil Connections," News and Trends North America, Volume 6 Issue 10, www.gasandoil.com/goc/news/ntn12276.htm. (Webpage identifies USATODAY.com as the original source.)

[109] *State of the World 2001*, Worldwatch Institute, page 43

[110] 1996 Footprint Data, WWF/UNEP-WCMC Living Planet Report 2000. Extrapolations to 2050 and 2100 are by the author, and are based on Census Bureau population projections. The extrapolations assume per capita consumption fixed at 1996 levels, and that total biological productivity remains fixed at 1996 level.

[111] *Earth Rising*, Phillip Shabecoff, 2000, page 20

[112] Letter to the Editor, *Washington Post*, June 3, 2001

[113] http://www.bot.org/html/biz/transportation-link.asp, June 2001

[114] Paraphrase from "The City as a Growth Machine," by Harvey Molotch, in *The American Journal of Sociology, 1976*

[115] Taken from *Better, Not Bigger*, by Eben Fodor, 1999, p29. Fodor cited *Regulation for Revenue* by Alan Altshuler and Jose Gomez-Ibanez, published by The Brookings Institution in 1993.

Endnotes 133

[116] *Changing Places*, Richard Moe and Carter Wilkie, Owl Books, 1997, page 34
[117] *Better, Not Bigger*, Eben Fodor, page 30. The content of this paragraph and the two that follow was substantially guided by the writing of Fodor and Molotch ("The City as Growth Machine").
[118] http://www.plannersweb.com/sprawl/roots_tax.html, June 2001
[119] The 1999 Loudon County, VA Board of Supervisors election is a case in point. See "In Busy Loudon, Building a Revolt," Justin Blum, *Washington Post*, November 24, 1999.
[120] "Maryland Businessman Ready to Run," Daniel LeDuc, *Washington Post*, June 20, 2001.
[121] For example: The Columbia Gorge Economic Development Association inserted a full page ad in the *2001 Gorge Guide*, proclaiming the Columbia River Gorge to be the ideal business environment.
[122] "Hey Silicon Valley, Get a Load of This", Kenneth Bredemeier, *The Washington Post*, April 17, 2000, Washington Business, page 5
[123] "$7 million buys Pa. Jobs for Md.," Jay Hancock, *Baltimore Sun*, October 11, 1999
[124] "Officials base subsidies on flawed model," Jay Hancock, *Baltimore Sun*, October 12, 1999.
[125] "Taxpayers get no voice in billions for businesses," Jay Hancock, *Baltimore Sun*, October 13, 1999
[126] Quoted in *Better, Not Bigger*, Eben Fodor, New Society Publishers, 1999, page 34
[127] "$7 million buys Pa. Jobs for Md.," Jay Hancock, *Baltimore Sun*, October 11, 1999.
[128] "Virginia Kills Plan to Let Localities Slow Growth," Justin Blum, *Washington Post*, February 9, 2000
[129] "As Far As The Eye Can See," Larry Van Dyne, *Washingtonian Magazine*, February 2000.
[130] "The Political Logic of Economic Development," Roland Stephen, Dept. of Political Science and Public Administration, North Carolina State University, http://www2.chass.ncsu.edu/stephen/pleddra.PDF
[131] "Economists split on biotech tax benefit," Steven Dennis, *Gaithersburg Gazette*, October 4, 2000
[132] Population Growth and the Environment – Revisited," Professor Albert Bartlett, University of Colorado, 1998, http://bcn.boulder.co.us/basin/local/bartlett.html

[133] "As Far As The Eye Can See," Larry Van Dyne, *Washingtonian Magazine*, February 2000

[134] Infrastructure Subsidies: $738 million; Economic Development Subsidies: $257 million; Subsidized Planning and Development Services: 33 million. *Assessment of Statewide Growth Subsidies in Oregon*, Fodor & Associates, February 2002, Table 9-1. Year 2000 population of Oregon was 3.41 million and the 1990 – 2000 change was 20.4%; U.S. Census Bureau (Quick Facts, www.census.gov) Using linear interpolation, the Year 2000 population increase is estimated to be about 58,000 people.

[135] The amount to assess each new facility would be in proportion to the number of new residents that would result from the new facility. New facilities constructed in brownfields areas would be exempted. It is important that the assessment be on new business facilities and not on new residences. Otherwise, the price of housing will escalate while new businesses growth continues to attract new residents.

[136] http://www.arch.virginia.edu/~plan/common/courses/plac/gm/mcma1.htm

[137] Virginia APF regulations are applicable only to rezoning applications.
http://www.arch.virginia.edu/~plan/common/courses/plac/gm/pf.htm

[138] CITPAC, http://users.rcn.com/wolff99/denis.htm

[139] Til Hazel quote about Agricultural Reserve in "Montgomery's Line of Defense Against Suburban Invasion," Stephen Fehr, *The Washington Post*, March 25, 1997

[140] "Developers Put Money On Duncan Reelection," Jo Becker, *The Washington Post*, November 10, 2001.

[141] "Md. Businessman Ready to Run," Daniel Leduc, *The Washington Post*, June 20, 2001. Also, "Go Montgomery, Transportation Plan for Our Future," Douglas Duncan, June 25, 2002

[142] 1998 net immigration: 0.96 million; estimated 2002 net immigration: 0.97 million, Table E; 1999 TFR: 2.047, Table B; "Methodology and Assumptions for the Population Projections of the United States," Population Division Working Paper No. 38, Census Bureau, January 13, 2000

[143] The upper curve uses the Census Bureau middle series total fertility rate (TFR) assumptions through the year 2100. While the demographic assumptions for this model are simpler than those used by the Census Bureau, the upper curve is a close approximation to the

Census Bureau middle series projection (0.3% at 2050 and 2.7% at 2100).
[144] *The State of the World Population 2000*, Demographic, Social, and Economic Indicators
[145] "A Smaller But Better Future," *Sierra*, The Magazine of the Sierra Club, July/August 1999
[146] *The State of the World Population 2000*, UNFPA, United Nations Population Fund, Demographic, Social, and Economic Indicators
[147] "Is Education the Best Contraceptive?" *MEASURE Communication*, Population Reference Bureau, May 2000
[148] *Fertility of American Women*, June 1995, Bureau of the Census, Table 2, Parts A-D
[149] *Statistical Abstracts of the United States, 2000*, Table No. 251
[150] *Fertility of American Women*, June 1995, Bureau of the Census, Table A
[151] *Misplaced Blame*, Alan Durning and Christopher Crowther, NEW Report Number 5, July 1997, pp 14, 15
[152] *Misplaced Blame*, Alan Durning and Christopher Crowther, NEW Report Number 5, July 1997, pp 13, 14
[153] "Highlights of Trends in Pregnancies and Pregnancy Rates by Outcome: Estimates for the United States 1976 – 1996," The Alan Guttmacher Institute, National Vital Statistics Reports, December 15, 1999
[154] "Trap door? Revolving Door? or Both?" Mary Naifeh, Current Population Reports, P70-63, US Census Bureau, July 1998
[155] *Misplaced Blame*, Alan Durning and Christopher Crowther, NEW Report Number 5, July 1997, p 29
[156] *Child Well-Being, Child Poverty and Child Policy in Modern Nations*, by Koen Vleminckx and Timothy M. Smeeding, The Maxwell School of Syracuse University, http://www.maxwell.syr.edu/deans/news/child_poverty_map.html
[157] The Sierra Club's Michael McCloskey required such a nexus in determining what social issues are appropriate for Sierra Club involvement; *Earth Rising*, by Philip Shabecoff, Island Press 2000, page 57
[158] "Achievements in Public Health 1900 - 1999, Family Planning," Morbidity and Mortality Weekly Report, December 3, 1999. http://www.cdc.gov/mmwr/PDF/wk/mm4847.pdf
[159] "The Family Planning Attitudes and Experiences of Low-income Women," Jacqueline Darroch Forrest and Jennifer J. Frost, Volume

28, No. 6, November/December 1996, http://www.agi-usa.org/pubs/journals/2824696.html

[160] *How America Views World Population Issues*, RAND Corp, March 2000, Chapter 5, Question 62

[161] The administration's plan to end contraceptive coverage was contained in Bush's $1.96 trillion budget proposal released April 2001.

[162] *How America Views World Population Issues*, RAND Corp, March 2000, Chapter 5, Question 63

[163] "More Companies Covering Contraception," Mary Deibel, Scripps Howard, published in the *Montgomery Journal* July 3, 2001

[164] "The Family Planning Attitudes and Experiences of Low-income Women," Jacqueline Darroch Forrest and Jennifer J. Frost, Volume 28, No. 6, November/December 1996, http://www.agi-usa.org/pubs/journals/2824696.html

[165] "A Smaller But Better Future," *Sierra*, The Magazine of the Sierra Club, July/August 1999

[166] "Highlights of Trends in Pregnancies and Pregnancy Rates by Outcome: Estimates for the U.S. 1976 – 1996," *National Vital Statistics Reports*, Volume 47, Number 29, December 1999

[167] *15th Anniversary*, Annual Report of Population Communications International Summer 2001

[168] This form of the equation assumes no changes in technology that would mitigate the environmental consequences of consumption, and is a simplified version of the famous equation. The actual equation presented by Ehrlich and Holdren is $I = P \times A \times T$; where A is affluence (consumption) and T is a technology multiplier. See "Impact of Population Growth," *Science*, vol. 171, 1974. The more general form of the equation is used in cases where the technology behind the consumption is relevant, e.g., consumption of energy from fossil fuels versus energy from solar or wind sources.

[169] For example, reliance on solar energy rather than fossil fuel or nuclear energy may permit increased power consumption without proportional environmental decline. See previous endnote.

[170] "The Environmental Movement's Retreat From Advocating U.S. Population Stabilization (1970 – 1998)," Roy Beck and Leon Kolankiewicz,

[171] Based on 2000 – 2050 percent change in population data provided by the Population Reference Bureau 2001 World Population Data

Endnotes 137

Sheet. Israel (with a population roughly the size of the Washington Metro Area) is the one exception with a projected increase of 64%.
[172] *Picture Maryland: Where do we GROW from here? A Citizen's guide to Shaping the Future of Maryland*, Maryland' Tributary Teams, no date
[173] *Ishmael*, Daniel Quinn, Bantam, 1995, page 37
[174] Bold, italicized type within quoted text in this appendix is added emphasis not in the original material.
[175] http://www.mdchamber.org/index2.html, June 2001
[176] http://www.pgcoc.org/, June 2001
[177] http://www.fccc.org/legislative/legislt.htm, June 2001
[178] To Cross the Potomac, *Washington Post*, June 5, page A20
[179] http://www.bot.org/membship.html (March 30, 2000)
[180] http://www.bot.org/html/members/committees/committees.asp (June 18, 2001)
[181] *Land Use in America*, Henry diamond and Patrick Noonan, Island Press 1996, page 177
[182] http://www.fairfaxcountyeda.org/, June 2001
[183] http://www.co.mo.md.us/government/omb/fy01approved/volume1/60.htm, June 2001
[184] "Population Projections of the United States by Age, Sex, Race, and Hispanic Origin: 1995 to 2050," P25-1130, Census Bureau, February 1996, Table E. Note: in P25-1130 the Census Bureau defines working age as 18 to 65.
[185] "Replacement Migration," United Nations Population Division, ESA/P/WP.160, 21 March 2000.
[186] "Replacement Migration," United Nations Population Division, ESA/P/WP.160, 21 March 2000, Chapter II, page 10.
[187] *Methodology and Assumptions for the Population Projections of the United States: 1999 – 2100*, Population Division Working Paper Number 38, U.S. Census Bureau, January 13, 2000, Table F.
[188] The values in Figure C-4 are based on an idealized population pyramid in which the number of persons in each age cohort is the same until age 65. Beyond age 65 the number decreases by a constant rate such that by the mean longevity age, the cohort is smaller by half, and zero at longevity + ten years. In comparing Figures C-4 and C-3, it should be noted that the Census Bureau longevity assumption for the Middle Series is 90 years.

[189] "Summary of Travel Trends 1995 Nationwide Personal Transportation Survey," December 1999, USDOT, Table 5. The travel categories included account for about 88% of household vehicular travel; the excluded categories are church, school, medical, and dental.

[190] "Summary of Travel Trends 1995 Nationwide Personal Transportation Survey," December 1999, USDOT, Tables 4 and 5.

[191] "Summary of Travel Trends 1995 Nationwide Personal Transportation Survey," December 1999, USDOT, page G-10.

[192] "Summary of Travel Trends 1995 Nationwide Personal Transportation Survey," December 1999, USDOT, Table 1.

[193] "Summary of Travel Trends 1995 Nationwide Personal Transportation Survey," December 1999, USDOT, Table 15.